P9-DFI-424

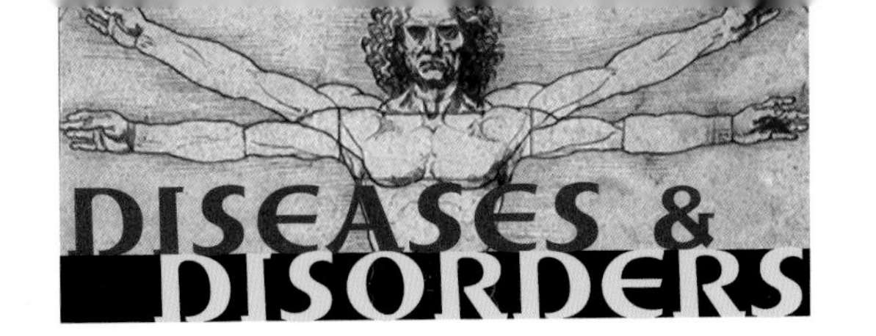

Allergies

Titles in the Diseases and Disorders series include:

Acne
AIDS
Alzheimer's Disease
Anorexia and Bulimia
Anthrax
Arthritis
Asthma
Attention Deficit Disorder
Autism
Bipolar Disorder
Birth Defects
Breast Cancer
Cerebral Palsy
Chronic Fatigue Syndrome
Cystic Fibrosis
Deafness
Diabetes
Down Syndrome
Dyslexia
Epilepsy
Fetal Alcohol Syndrome
Food Poisoning
Growth Disorders
Headaches
Heart Disease
Hemophilia
Hepatitis
Human Papillomavirus (HPV)
Leukemia
Lou Gehrig's Disease
Lyme Disease
Mad Cow Disease
Malaria
Malnutrition
Measles and Rubella
Meningitis
Mental Retardation
Multiple Sclerosis
Obesity
Ovarian Cancer
Parkinson's Disease
Phobias
SARS
Schizophrenia
Sexually Transmitted Diseases
Sleep Disorders
Smallpox
Strokes
Teen Depression
Toxic Shock Syndrome
Tuberculosis
West Nile Virus

Allergies

Barbara Sheen

LUCENT BOOKS
A part of Gale, Cengage Learning

Detroit • New York • San Francisco • New Haven, Conn • Waterville, Maine • London

LIBRARY OF CONGRESS CATALOGING-IN-PUBLICATION DATA

Sheen, Barbara.
Allergies / by Barbara Sheen.
p. cm. — (Diseases & disorders)
Includes bibliographical references and index.
ISBN 978-1-4205-0039-4 (hardcover)
1. Allergy—Juvenile literature. I. Title.
RC585.S52 2008
616.97—dc22

2008003798

Lucent Books
27500 Drake Rd
Farmington Hills MI 48331

ISBN-13: 978-1-4205-0039-4
ISBN-10: 1-4205-0039-2

Printed in the United States of America
1 2 3 4 5 6 7 12 11 10 09 08

Table of Contents

Foreword 6

Introduction
A Widespread Problem 8

Chapter 1
What Are Allergies? 13

Chapter 2
Diagnosis and Conventional Treatment 28

Chapter 3
Alternative and Complementary Treatments 43

Chapter 4
Living with Allergies 59

Chapter 5
The Future of Allergies 74

Notes 88

Glossary 93

Organizations to Contact 96

For Further Reading 98

Index 100

Picture Credits 104

About the Author 104

FOREWORD

"The Most Difficult Puzzles Ever Devised"

Charles Best, one of the pioneers in the search for a cure for diabetes, once explained what intrigued him so about medical research: "It's not just the gratification of knowing one is helping people," he confided, "although that probably is a more heroic and selfless motivation. Those feelings may enter in, but truly, what I find best is the feeling of going toe to toe with nature, of trying to solve the most difficult puzzles ever devised. The answers are there somewhere, those keys that will solve the puzzle and make the patient well. But how will those keys be found?"

Since the dawn of civilization, nothing has so puzzled people—and often frightened them, as well—as the onset of illness in a body or mind that seemed healthy before. Being unable to reverse conditions such as a seizure, the inability of a heart to pump, or the sudden deterioration of muscle tone in a small child, or even to understand why they occur was unspeakably frustrating to healers. Even before there were names for such conditions, before they were understood at all, each was a reminder of how complex the human body was and how vulnerable.

While our grappling with understanding diseases has been frustrating at times, it has also provided some of humankind's most heroic accomplishments. Alexander Fleming's accidental discovery in 1928 of a mold that could be turned into penicillin has resulted in the saving of untold millions of lives. The isolation of the enzyme insulin has reversed what was once a death sentence for anyone with diabetes. There also have been great strides in combating conditions for which there is not yet a cure. Medicines can help AIDS patients live longer, diagnostic tools such as mammography and ultrasounds can help doctors find tumors while they are treatable, and laser surgery techniques have made the most intricate, minute operations routine.

This "toe-to-toe" competition with diseases and disorders is even more remarkable when viewed in a historical continuum. An astonishing amount of progress has been made in a very short time. Just two hundred years ago, the existence of germs as a cause of some diseases was unknown. In fact, less than 150 years ago a British surgeon named Joseph Lister had difficulty persuading his fellow doctors that washing their hands before delivering a baby might increase the chances of a healthy delivery (especially if they had just attended to a diseased patient)!

Each book in Lucent's Diseases and Disorders series explores a disease or disorder and the knowledge that has been accumulated (or discarded) by doctors through the years. Each book also examines the tools used for pinpointing a diagnosis, as well as the various means that are used to treat or cure a disease. Finally, new ideas are presented—techniques or medicines that may be on the horizon.

Frustration and disappointment are still part of medicine because not every disease or condition can be cured or prevented. But the limitations of knowledge are constantly being pushed outward; the "most difficult puzzles ever devised" are finding challengers every day.

INTRODUCTION

A Widespread Problem

A young woman joined her friends for a meal in a college dining room. She had only taken a few bites when she started feeling ill. "My lips started to swell and my whole body was itching, and I was sweating like crazy," she recalls. " I was getting weak and threw up a couple of times…. At this point I couldn't think. I couldn't talk (my mouth and tongue were swelling) and I just couldn't stop crying…. I felt like my hands and feet were starting to shake like they were being electrocuted, and my stomach started to cramp."[1]

The young woman had unknowingly eaten a peanut, a food that she was highly allergic to. Without prompt treatment, the results could have been deadly. And what happened to this young woman was not an isolated incident.

Not a Trivial Problem

There is a widespread belief that allergies are seasonal nuisances, causing no more trouble than the common cold. This is not true. In any given year in the United States, allergies account for more than thirty thousand emergency room visits and an estimated seven hundred deaths.

Even when allergy cases do not require hospitalization or threaten lives, they do produce unpleasant symptoms that can make allergy sufferers feel unwell, worsen other health con-

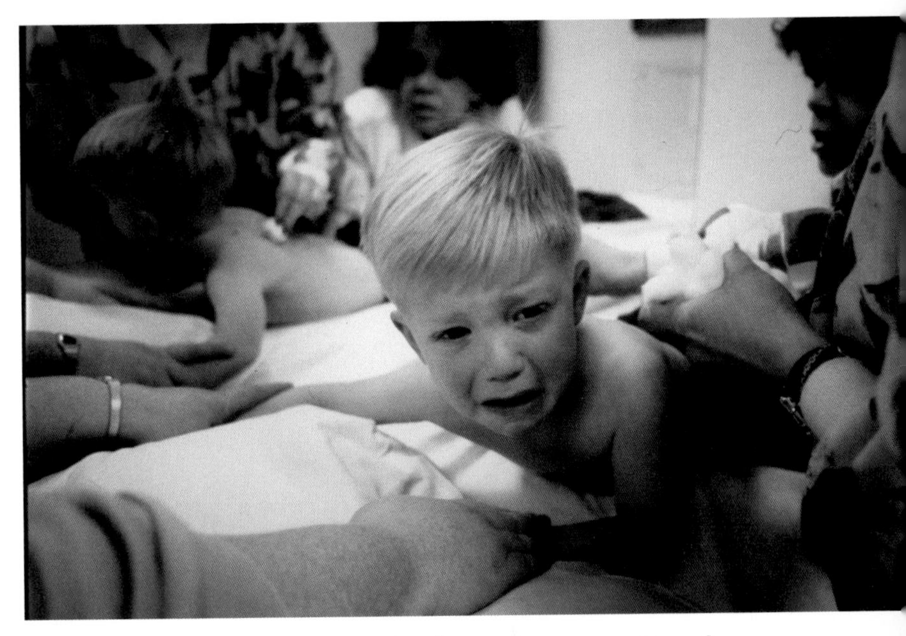

Allergies can have serious, even deadly, consequences. Here four-year-old Jeremiah Jager undergoes an allergen test to try and determine the cause of respiratory and allergy problems that have already hospitalized him eight times in his short life.

ditions, and/or cause secondary illnesses to develop. In some instances allergies—especially those to food, insect venom, and medications—can be deadly. Author and allergy expert Earl Mindell explains:

> Allergy is not a trivial problem. First and foremost, allergies can make people miserable.... Allergies may threaten our health in ways that are not quite fully understood. For example, some studies suggest that unrecognized food allergies may be linked to numerous medical conditions such as Chronic Obstructive Pulmonary Disease [an illness that affects a person's ability to breathe], rheumatoid arthritis, an autoimmune disease in which the immune cells attack the joints, Attention Deficit Disorder in children, and even migraine headaches. Allergic rhinitis (a fancy name for the stuffy, itchy nose caused

by hay fever) is a leading cause of recurrent sinusitis or sinus infections, an inflammation of the sinus membranes that plagues tens of millions of people and leads to sinus surgery.[2]

More Cases

Making matters worse, the number of people throughout the world with allergies has more than doubled within the last fifty years. According to Dr. Scott H. Sicherer of Mount Sinai Hospital in New York City, "We're basically looking at what may be a public-health crisis."[3]

Currently, an estimated 50 million people in the United States have allergies. That translates to 20 percent of all Americans. From 15 to 30 percent of all Europeans are allergy sufferers, too. And these numbers are growing. According to the European Commission, a group concerned with European health issues, by 2015, 50 percent of all Europeans will have allergies. Experts in the United States predict a similar growth pattern.

Test strips containing different allergens are applied to the back of this patient by her dermatologist as part of a test to determine what allergies she has.

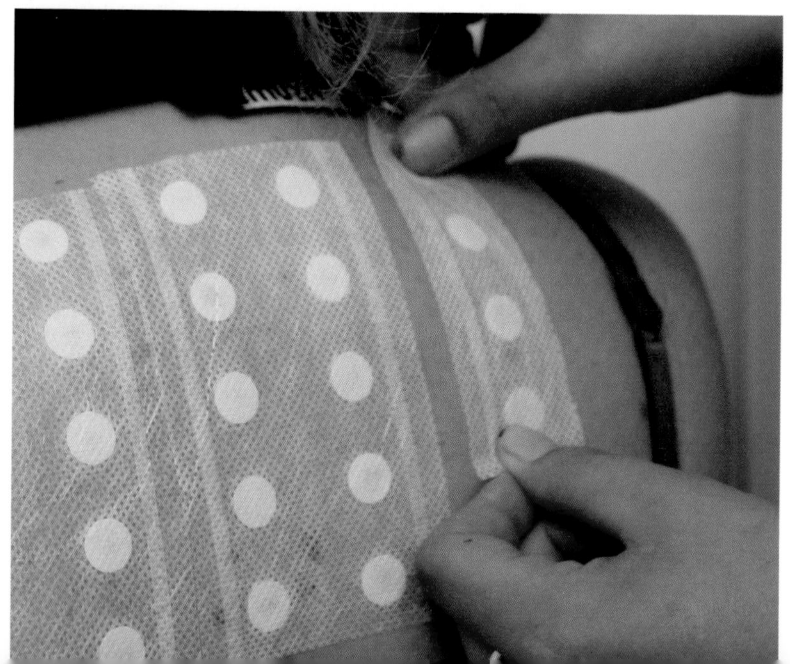

A 2005 study conducted jointly by the National Institute of Environmental and Health Sciences and the National Institute of Allergy and Infectious Diseases showed how vulnerable people are to allergies. Researchers exposed the skin of 10,500 individuals aged six to fifty-nine to the ten most common allergens (normally harmless substances such as pollen or dust that cause some people to experience allergic reactions) then measured their reactions. Fifty-four percent of the subjects were sensitive to at least one allergen. This means that more than half the subjects were already allergic to at least one allergen or are at risk of developing such an allergy in the future. The scientists say that because the test only looked at ten allergens (and there are actually thousands), if the subjects were exposed to more allergens the reaction rate would probably be quite a bit higher. Since the subjects represented a cross section of typical Americans, if the total population of the United States were tested in the same way, the results would be similar. Interestingly, when the same test was conducted thirty years earlier, only 27 percent of the subjects reacted, an indicator of how vulnerability to allergies has increased.

Economic and Social Costs

Because the incidence of allergies is so widespread, the condition has a substantial impact on society, burdening the health-care system, decreasing work and school productivity, and negatively affecting the quality of life of allergy sufferers. According to the National Institutes of Health, allergies are the fifth leading chronic disease in the United States, and the third most common in American children under the age of eighteen. An estimated 16.7 million visits to doctors' offices each year are due to allergies. The cost of these visits combined with the cost of allergy medications comes to $4.8 billion annually.

Allergies also cause absenteeism in students and workers. American students miss approximately 2 million school days each year due to allergies. That translates to ten thousand absences per day. American workers miss 1.8 million workdays annually due to allergies.

Even when students and workers go to school or work on days when they are suffering from allergy symptoms, their symptoms impair their ability to function well, causing their productivity to drop significantly. According to allergy specialist Dr. Richard Page of Garland, Texas, people with allergies "have less energy, and difficulty concentrating."[4] Also, many allergy medications cause drowsiness, raising safety issues in the workplace. A 1996 Seattle study found that workers taking sedating medications, such as those used to control allergy symptoms, are one and a half times more likely to have a workplace accident than are other workers.

Altogether, the problems allergies cause in the workplace cost Americans an estimated $4 billion a year. Frank Brocato, president of the Employer Health Coalition Inc., a group that looks at workplace health and safety issues, explains: "That amount is far greater than productivity loss associated with such conditions as hypertension, diabetes, heart disease, and breast cancer."[5]

Importance of Knowledge

In light of the considerable impact allergies have on individuals and society, it is not sensible or safe to dismiss allergies as simply a nuisance. By learning ways to manage and control their allergies, individuals with allergies can improve the quality of their lives. And when friends, family members, and coworkers learn more about allergies, they know how to provide allergy sufferers with appropriate support. In some cases, such knowledge can be a lifesaver. Alyssa, who has a severe milk allergy, puts it this way: "People without allergies should be knowledgeable on the signs of a reaction, know the different medications, and know how to help. If more non-allergic people understood … allergies, they would be more likely to help when an allergic person has a reaction."[6]

What Are Allergies?

An allergy is a hypersensitivity disorder. Allergic individuals are overly sensitive to one or more allergens, normally harmless substances that do not cause problems in most other people. This sensitivity causes the immune system to overreact. This overreaction makes people with allergies feel ill. Common allergens include pollen, mold, pet dander, insect venom, latex, drugs, and many foods, to name just a few.

Allergies and the Immune System

The immune system consists of billions of specialized cells that protect the body from harmful foreign substances like bacteria, viruses, fungi, and parasites. Through a series of steps called an immune response, the immune system determines the identity of a foreign invader, establishes whether it is harmful, and then, if the invader is identified as a threat, launches an attack against it.

When a foreign substance enters the body, white blood cells called lymphocytes are sent to the area. When they come in contact with the invader, they engulf it. This causes bits of the foreign substance's surface protein to stick to the lymphocytes. The composition of the protein alerts the immune system to the identity of the invader.

If the invader is identified as an antigen, a dangerous foreign substance, the immune system releases specialized proteins known as antibodies. The body produces millions of different antibodies; each shaped to match up with and lock on to a specific antigen. When an antibody locks on to an antigen, it

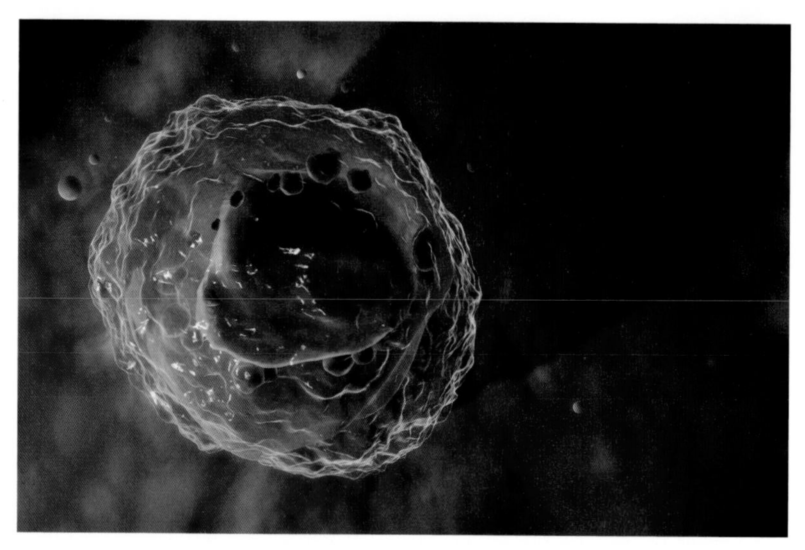

Lymphocytes like this white blood cell defend the body against diseases, but sometimes react to harmless substances as well, causing an allergic response.

releases powerful chemicals that destroy the antigen; however, the first time the body is exposed to a particular antigen, it takes about two weeks for the immune system to manufacture the appropriate antibodies. Thereafter, the immune system is always on guard against that particular antigen.

In the case of allergies, the immune system mistakenly identifies a harmless substance such as grass pollen for a dangerous invader. The first time the body is exposed to that allergen, the immune system begins manufacturing an antibody known as immunoglobulin E (IgE). As with all antibody production, it takes the immune system at least two weeks to produce the specific IgE antibody that matches the allergen.

Once the antibody is produced, it attaches to mast cells. These are cells that line the nose, throat, lungs, skin, and gastrointestinal tract, the areas of the body in which allergens settle. The next time the allergen enters the body, IgE locks on to it. This activates the mast cells, triggering the release of chemicals contained within them. This process is known as allergic sensitization.

The Immune System

The immune system is the body's defense system against disease. White blood cells are the key to this system. There are many types of white blood cells. They work together to fight harmful microorganisms. Each has a specific job.

Neutrophils are the most common type of white blood cell. Their job is to fight bacteria. Dead neutrophils are what make up pus.

Eosinophils and basophils are less common. Eosinophils attack parasites in the skin and the lungs. Basophils are involved in causing inflammation.

Lymphocytes focus on viruses and bacteria. There are two types of lymphocytes: T cells and B cells. B cells produce antibodies. T cells identify antigens and signal the release of antibodies. Along with antibodies, T cells attack the threatening substance, which in the case of allergies is not threatening at all, but rather, a harmless allergen.

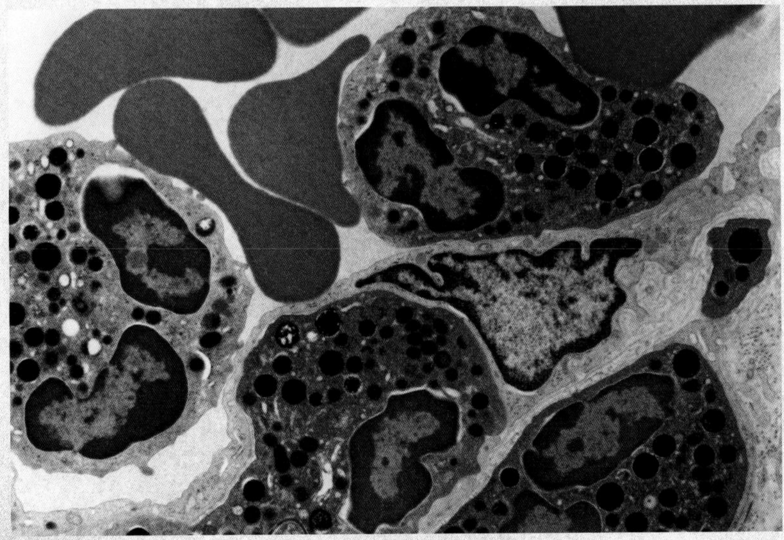

The most common type of white blood cell is a neutrophil. Neutrophils fight bacteria.

An Allergic Reaction

Histamine is one of the chemicals the mast cells release. Its release, along with the release of other powerful chemicals, causes inflammation, which is one of the body's ways of fighting harmful organisms. But when no actual threat to the body exists, as in the case of allergies, inflammation sets off a chain of events that causes problems. First, in order to get blood and immune cells to the affected area, inflammation causes blood vessels to widen. As a result, blood floods into the affected area, causing redness. As blood and immune cells leak into nearby tissues, swelling develops. When swollen tissues press on nearby nerve endings, irritation, itching, and/or pain develops. Authors Dr. Frank K. Kwong and Bruce W. Cook describe what happens when an inhaled allergen triggers an allergic reaction in the nose: "The substance histamine will cause the rich supply of blood vessels in the nose to become leaky. Imagine many holes punched in the plumbing of your house. Fluid will gush out of the blood capillaries to cause edema [swelling] in your nose."[7]

Similarly, if the allergen enters the body through the skin, the results are likely to include itching, redness, swelling, and hives. If the allergen enters through the mouth, the lips and tongue swell. If it enters through the nose, the swelling of the mucous membranes and blood vessels lining the nose and sinuses cause a feeling of fullness. Histamine also stimulates the manufacture and release of mucus, a substance that traps harmful irritants. Depending on where the allergen triggers a reaction, excess mucus can cause a runny nose, watery eyes, and/or airway congestion.

Making matters worse, inflammation causes the smooth muscles in the airways to constrict, which leads to wheezing and difficulty breathing. Inflammation also prompts the body to try to expel harmful substances in the form of sneezing, coughing, vomiting, and diarrhea. It is the release of histamine and the accompanying inflammation that defines an allergic reaction. It is this reaction, not the allergen itself, that makes people feel ill. John, who is allergic to a number of substances, including

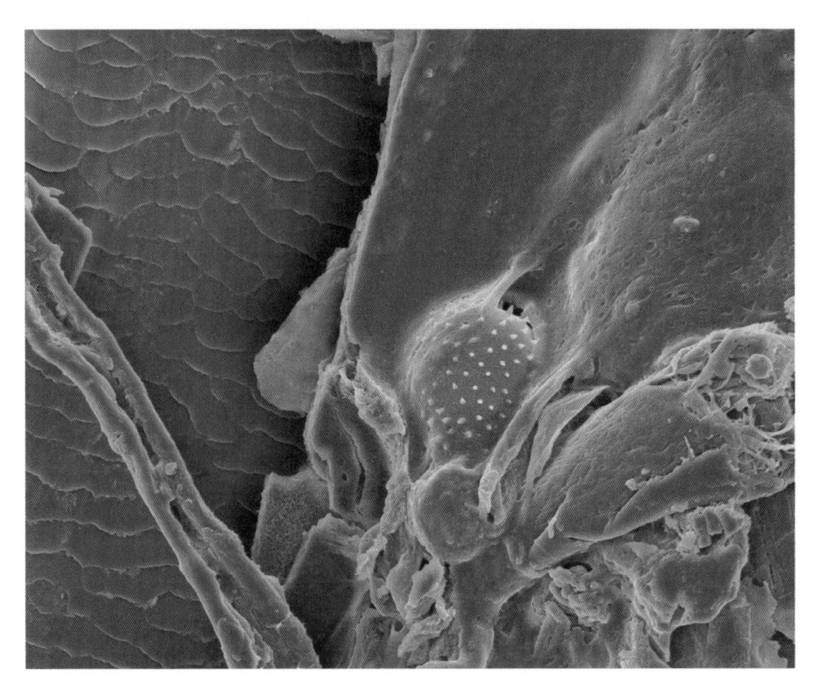

A magnified view of the inside of a nose shows a grain of pollen trapped in mucus near a nose hair. During an allergic reaction the body often produces excessive and uncomfortable amounts of mucus.

ragweed pollen, explains: "Some people can be around ragweed and it doesn't bother them. When I'm around it, it makes me sneeze and my nose run. I know ragweed is harmless, but the way my body reacts to it makes it annoying to me."[8]

Different Allergens

Inflammation and the problems it causes can be triggered by thousands of different allergens. The body can produce a huge array of IgE antibodies, each specific to a different allergen. Consequently, individuals can be allergic to many different substances. Melissa, an allergy sufferer, explains: "I'm allergic to tree nuts, (not peanuts—that's a legume), roses, different grasses, dogs and cats."[9]

To make distinguishing between the many different allergens simpler, they are often classified by the way they enter the

Poplar wool hangs in the air over a street in Moscow, Russia. The wool, similar to dandelion fluff, coats the city for several weeks every year, bringing misery for allergy sufferers.

body. They can be inhaled, ingested, or enter the body through the skin. Allergens that are inhaled are carried in the air and enter the body through an individual's nose or mouth. They are among the most common substances that trigger an allergic reaction and include plant pollens, mold, dust mites, and pet dander, to name a few.

Often, pollen allergies are seasonal. In temperate climates, most plants and trees release a high level of pollen into the air during warm weather. The abundance of pollen circulating through the air at this time causes people with pollen allergies to become ill. During the winter, most plants and trees are dormant and do not release pollen. Consequently, individuals with seasonal allergies feel well then. "As far as my pollen allergies," John explains, "they bother me in June and July. The rest of the year, especially once we get a hard freeze, I hardly notice them."[10]

Seasonal pollen allergies are more popularly known as hay fever. Hay fever usually causes allergic rhinitis, or nasal inflammation. It is the most common allergic condition in the United States, affecting an estimated 45 million people. According to Dr. Beth Corn of Mount Sinai Hospital in New York City, "Hay fever is usually what presents in the springtime. And the reason it has this name is because about 150 years ago, the hay harvesting season was in the spring and so people thought the symptoms were from hay. But, in actuality, the symptoms are caused by grass and trees."[11]

Other Inhalant Allergies

Other inhalant allergies, such as those to dust or pet dander, affect people year round because these substances are always circulating in the air. Dust is composed of tiny particles of different substances, any of which can prompt an allergic response. These substances include mold spores and dust mites. The latter are microscopic spiderlike creatures whose droppings are among the most common allergy triggers. In addition to

This is a magnified view of a dust mite, which is roughly .01 inch across. Dust mites are common in homes, and many people are allergic to their droppings.

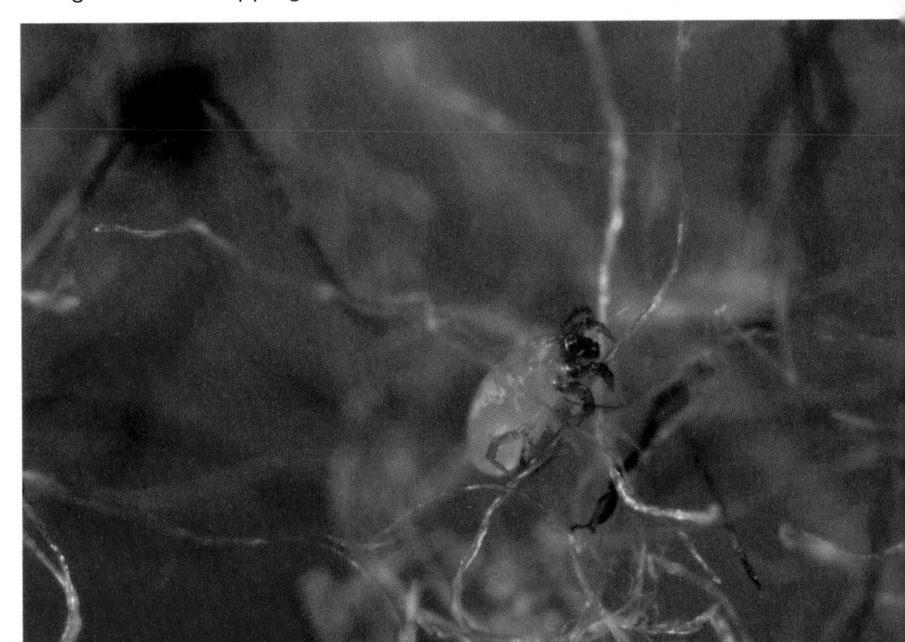

being found in dust, dust mites live inside pillows, mattresses, curtains, upholstered furniture, and rugs and can be carried around on clothing.

Pet dander is another common allergen. It is made up of proteins found in an animal's (such as a cat's or dog's) saliva, hair, and skin. Pet dander is extremely small. A particle of cat dander can be as small as a half a micron. (One micron is equal to a thousandth of a millimeter.) Pet dander is so tiny that particles of it can hang in unmoving air for up to six hours. The slightest movement gets the particles circulating.

Although individuals can be sensitive to all types of pet dander, cat dander allergies are the most common. Sam and his wife are both allergic to cat dander: "My wife knew she didn't feel quite right, but wasn't sure why. She did not like it when I suggested that her two cats might be the problem. For me, this was obvious, but to her the idea was brand new….I convinced her to see an allergist, and now we both get allergy shots."[12]

Contact Allergies

Other allergens enter the body through the skin. Depending on the allergen, these allergies can be year round or seasonal. For instance, people who are especially sensitive to certain plants may develop an allergic reaction when pollen or resins from these plants touch their skin. For such individuals sitting in a grassy field, for example, can cause them to develop an itchy rash. Such a response is likely to be seasonal.

Other allergens that enter through the skin can cause trouble year round. These include latex; proteins in different fibers, such as burlap, wool, or silk; and a wide array of chemicals found in grooming and cleaning products. This is how an allergen in nail polish affected Barbara: "I got this terrible itchy rash on my face, worst of all on my eyelids. It was a reaction to nail polish…. It was where I had been touching my face."[13] When allergies cause skin problems such as Barbara's, it is known as allergic dermatitis.

Chemicals contained in insect venom also enter the body through the skin and can cause an allergic reaction in sensi-

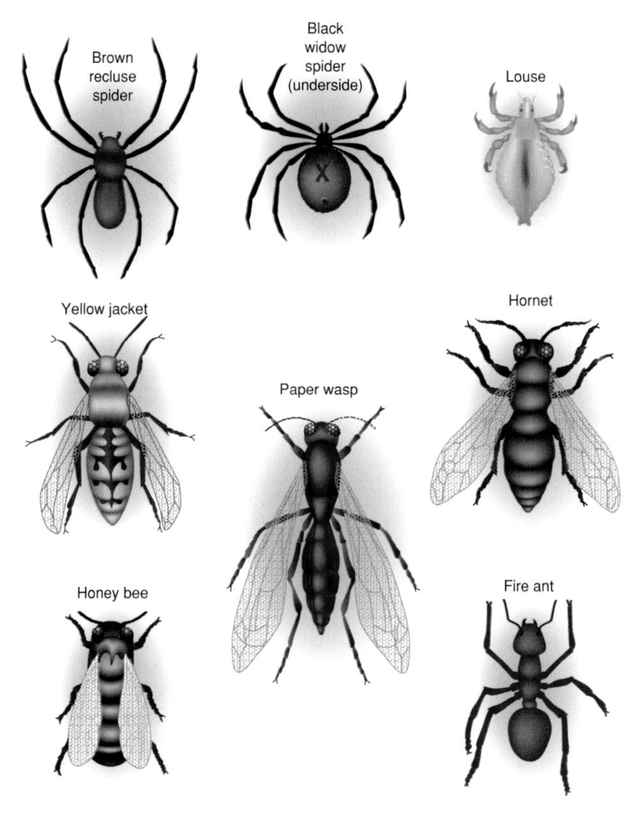

This chart shows the different types of poisonous spiders and bees, as well as a fire ant and a louse.

tive individuals. Wasps, honeybees, hornets, fire ants, and yellow jackets are the most common stinging insects that people react to. Usually, such stings cause pain, swelling, and itching in the affected area. But because an insect sting delivers allergens directly into an individual's bloodstream, it can cause a systemic, or full body, response. Such a response produces inflammation throughout the body and can be potentially life threatening. About 3 percent of children and 1 percent of adults in the United States experience this type of response. Hilary is one of them. She describes her response to a bee sting: "I started to itch like mad, all down my body. I felt sick and it was hard to breathe or talk. I went dizzy, and the next thing I knew, I woke up in a hospital."[14]

Ingested allergens

Drugs that are administered via injection have a similar effect on highly sensitive people. So do drugs that are ingested. Penicillin and related medications, sulfa drugs, and cephalosporin are frequent allergy triggers, as is aspirin. Certain foods, too, can induce a serious reaction in highly sensitive individuals. An estimated 7 million to 12 million Americans have food allergies. Although allergic reactions to food often involve allergic dermatitis or digestive tract problems, for those who are most sensitive, ingesting, or even inhaling, a microscopic bit of a particular food can provoke a potentially lethal systemic reaction.

Any food can act as an allergen, but peanuts, tree nuts, wheat, milk, eggs, fish, shellfish, and soy are the eight most popular food allergens. They cause 90 percent of all food allergies, with peanuts ranking as the leading cause of food allergies. Moreover, even individuals who do not have food allergies sometimes react to food. This is because certain pollens share similar proteins with certain foods. For instance, ragweed pol-

Eggs, fish, milk, peanuts, soy, tree nuts, and wheat are among the most common food allergens.

len shares similar proteins with watermelons, cantaloupes, and bananas. When individuals who are allergic to ragweed eat these foods, their immune systems may mistake the proteins for that of ragweed and launch an attack. This is more likely to happen if ragweed allergens are also present in the body, or if large quantities of the food are consumed. This type of reaction is known as cross- reactivity. In addition, many fruits, such as peaches, cherries, and apricots, cross-react with each other, so if individuals are allergic to one, they are likely to react to the others as well.

Atopic People

No matter the allergen, anyone can develop an allergy. Due to genetics, some people are more prone to developing allergies than are other people. Such people are said to be atopic; that means they are genetically predisposed to developing an allergy. This predisposition is passed down in a person's DNA from parent to child, making the tendency to develop allergies run in families.

Those individuals with a family history of allergies are most at risk. If a child has one parent with an allergy, that child has a 20 to 58 percent chance of also having an allergy. If both parents have an allergy, the number increases to 50 to 80 percent. The variation in the percentages is due to the fact that more than twenty genes are involved in atopy, the condition of being atopic. The more of these genes a person inherits, the greater his or her susceptibility to allergies. Janey comes from an atopic family. She explains:

> "My father had asthma [a respiratory disorder that is usually caused by allergies] as a child, and his sister had it too. In fact she died from it. My mother has never had any allergies, but one of her brothers had terrible hay fever all his life. Out of us four, only my brother, Peter, is completely allergy-free. I had bad eczema [a skin condition associated with allergic dermatitis] when I was small, as did my sister. So, when our son developed eczema, and

What Causes Shock?

When anaphylaxis occurs, shock can follow. During a severe allergic reaction, blood that would normally circulate throughout the body is diverted to and pools in the area where the allergen entered the body. This reduces the amount of blood circulating through the rest of the body. As a result, blood pressure drops.

Blood pressure is created as the heart pumps blood into the arteries, making the artery walls expand. The less blood the heart has to pump, the lower the pressure. With low blood pressure, the heart can pump only slowly and with less force than it normally does. Thus, less blood is pumped to the body. The vital organs become starved for the oxygen and nutrients that blood delivers. As a result, they cannot function properly. If normal blood pressure is not reestablished, the body goes into shock.

Shock is characterized by confusion, weakness, dizziness, a rapid pulse rate caused by the heart beating faster in an effort to raise blood pressure, and rapid breathing, which is the body's way to draw oxygen into the bloodstream. If shock is not treated, lack of blood can cause multiple organs to fail. Once this occurs, death follows.

then asthma, and an allergy to dust mites that made his nose run all the time, I wasn't entirely surprised.[15]

Interestingly, although people inherit the tendency to develop allergies, they do not inherit an allergy to a particular substance. Scientists do not know why this is so. According to Dr. Gillian Shepard at New York's Presbyterian Hospital, "It's an inherited tendency, but you don't specifically inherit an allergy to penicillin, or an allergy to grass pollen. You inherit a general tendency of the immune system to overreact."[16]

What's more, a person can be atopic but not develop allergy symptoms early on. Conditions in the immune system are always changing, making it possible for people to develop an allergy or stop reacting to a particular allergen at any point in their lives. In general, food allergies are more common in children than in adults. While hay fever and insect allergies usually make their first appearance during the teen years, drug allergies often develop in middle-aged adults. John explains: "I don't remember being allergic to any drugs as a kid. But when I was about 35, I had an allergic reaction to an antibiotic. A few years later, I was bit by a stray dog and had to get rabies shots. The shots caused my mouth and tongue to swell up. Then this year I had a horrible allergic reaction to another drug. It seems like the older I get, the worse I react to different drugs."[17]

The Role of the Environment

Moreover, some atopic people live their entire life without developing an allergy, while other people with no family history of allergies develop multiple allergies. Scientists do not know why this is so. They do know that an individual must be exposed to an allergen for symptoms to arise, and the more intense and frequent the exposure, the more likely it is that an allergy will develop. For this reason, people often develop

After he began getting allergic rashes on his hands, dentist Phil Hadley began wearing cloth liners to protect his skin from the latex gloves he uses at work. This is known as an occupational allergy.

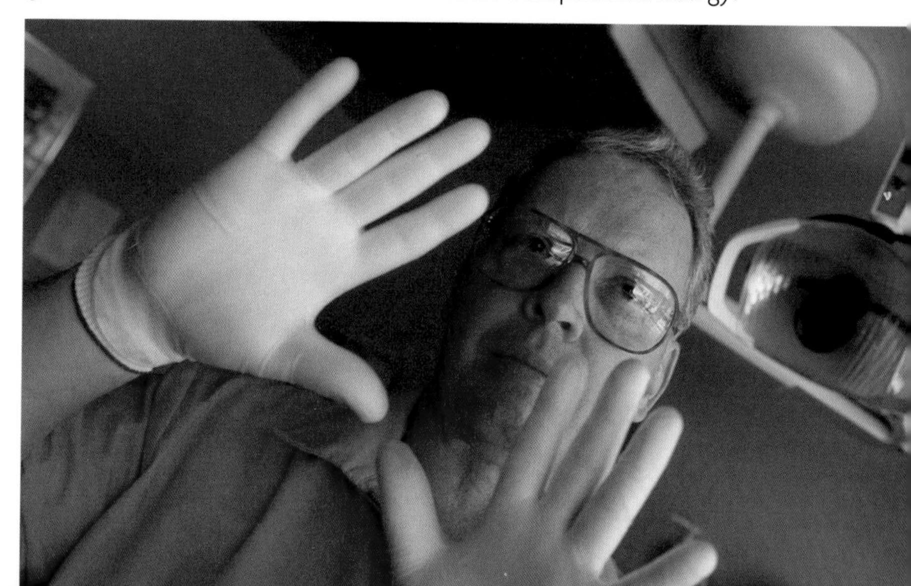

sensitivities to materials they work with. This is known as an occupational allergy. For instance, bakers are susceptible to allergies to wheat protein in flour, carpenters and sawmill workers to wood dust, hairdressers to dyes and chemicals, hospital workers to latex, and metal-industry workers to substances like cobalt and nickel. In general, symptoms flare up when sensitive individuals are at work and subside when they leave the work environment. Dale, a physician, explains how an occupational allergy to the powder inside latex gloves affected him: "Whenever anyone in the [operating room] would put on or remove their gloves that powder would fly and I would start to wheeze."[18]

When Allergies Threaten Lives

Dale's symptoms became so problematic that they affected his ability to breathe, forcing him to change professions. Indeed, if the inflammatory response that provokes allergy symptoms is not controlled, it can cause a number of health issues. Many people develop secondary conditions as a result. For example, overproduction of mucus can cause blockages in the sinuses, ears, and airways. Bacteria thrive in such an environment, leading to sinus and ear infections.

Asthma is another condition linked to allergies. It occurs when excess mucus forms into hard plugs in the lungs, causing breathing problems. Ninety percent of children with asthma and 70 percent of adults with the condition have allergies. Author Betty B. Wray, MD, describes how allergies affect her patient Malcolm: "He has an intense allergic reaction to cats and dogs. Just being in the same room where a pet has been can make Malcolm's throat close up. A minute later he's coughing up mucus, and sometimes his chest constricts, and an asthma attack threatens."[19]

More troubling, if allergy symptoms are severe and worsen rapidly, anaphylaxis can occur. Anaphylaxis is a systemic response to allergens in a person's bloodstream. It is most likely to be caused by food, insect venom, or drug allergens. Anaphylaxis involves the release of histamine and other inflammatory chemicals throughout the body. It usually begins with hives, the swelling of the tongue and throat, and breathing problems. If anaphylaxis is not controlled, it causes a dangerous drop in blood pressure that produces shock.

Shock is a medical emergency caused by the collapse of the circulatory system. If shock is not treated rapidly, death occurs. What makes anaphylaxis especially frightening is that it takes less than an hour from the time an allergen enters an affected individual's body for fatal symptoms to arise.

Although most people with allergies do not experience anaphylaxis, whenever an allergic reaction occurs, the results are unpleasant. The troubling reality is that any number of harmless substances can trigger the immune system to overreact. The resultant inflammation produces a wide variety of symptoms. For those with severe allergies, the results can be dangerous.

CHAPTER TWO

Diagnosis and Conventional Treatment

Diagnosing allergies involves identifying the particular allergen or allergens an individual reacts to. In some cases, this can be done by looking at an individual's medical history and administering a medical exam. Other cases are more difficult to pinpoint. Allergy testing can provide answers. Once the triggering allergen is identified, if it is possible for the patient to avoid the offending substance, no treatment is required. When avoidance is not possible, a number of different treatments are available. Which is best depends on the patient and the severity of the allergy. No treatment is without risk, however. As with all medications, those used to treat allergies can cause side effects.

Identifying Allergy Triggers

When a patient complains of allergy symptoms, the physician must determine whether the problem is an illness such as a cold, flu, or sinus infection, which produce symptoms similar to that of an allergy, or whether the problem is indeed an allergy. Administering a physical exam and taking the patient's medical history is the first step. Something as simple as the patient's temperature can help the doctor distinguish between the flu,

A woman runs down a path surrounded by ragweed and other plants. Pollen from plants is a common cause of allergies.

which causes fever, and an allergy, which usually does not. The duration of the individual's symptoms is also important. Cold and flu symptoms last about a week, but allergy symptoms can persist for months. Patients are also asked whether allergies run in their family. If the answer is yes, the physician knows that the patient is vulnerable to allergies.

If it appears that the problem is an allergy, it is essential to establish the triggering allergen. Once this is known, the patient can take steps to avoid exposure to the substance. When avoidance is not practical, treatment based on the triggering allergens can be administered. Other questions to determine whether the symptoms are associated with a particular activity or time of year, such as eating a certain food, petting a cat, or cutting the grass, to name a few possibilities, help the physician identify the triggering allergen and establish whether the problem is seasonal or year-round. Making a diagnosis and identifying the offending allergen in this manner may not provide an accurate picture of the condition. But if the allergy is seasonal, fairly mild, and not caused by multiple allergens, this type of diagnosis can be effective. Says Mindell, "You sneeze every time you're near a cat; your throat gets itchy after you eat a peanut; or your eyes start to tear every May at the start of hay fever season. Sometimes figuring out whether you are allergic to something is a 'no brainer.'"[20]

Skin Tests

Sometimes identifying triggering allergens can be more difficult, especially in cases of year-round or multiple allergies. In these cases, an allergy test is the best diagnostic tool. It can identify what allergens trigger an allergic reaction in affected individuals. According to Katy Weaver, an allergy sufferer and health writer, "It's difficult to find an unfamiliar destination without a road map. It's hard to hit a target unless you know

Allergens are applied to a patient's arm as part of an allergy test at a clinic in Heidelberg, Germany, in 2007.

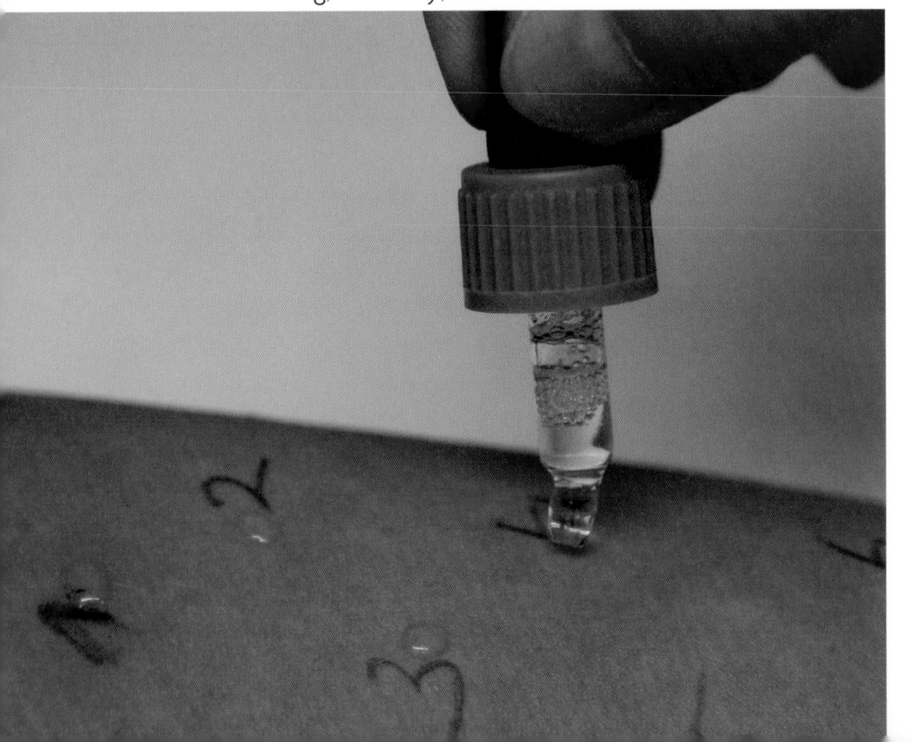

where you are aiming. Likewise, it's hard to find long-term allergy relief without knowing what to change or eliminate. Allergists administer allergy tests so they can have a specific action plan to help you with your allergies."[21]

The most common test is a skin prick or scratch test. It involves exposing the skin to different allergens and then observing the body's reaction. During a skin test, a health-care professional applies small drops of diluted extracts of different allergens to tiny scratches on the patient's forearm or upper back. As many as seventy allergens may be applied during one test and may include various plant and tree pollens, mold, dust, pet dander, wood pulp, insect venom, and different foods, to name just a few. The test is effective and shows sensitivity even to allergens that are usually inhaled. The allergens included in the test largely depend on the individuals tested, their medical history, and the types of allergens they are regularly exposed to. For instance, allergy tests in the southwestern United States typically include the pollen extracts of many desert plants. Such pollens, however, are not tested in the Northeast, where the plants that produce them are rare. John, who lives in New Mexico, explains: "Besides being tested for dust and different weeds and grasses, I was tested for mesquite trees, desert willows, and cactus. I was also tested for pecan trees and a bunch of other pollens like chile, cotton, and corn, because they grow in the area."[22]

Before the extracts are applied, the health-care professional cleanses the patient's skin with alcohol and then makes small marks on the patient's skin. A drop of a different allergen is applied to each mark. Then a small surgical instrument known as a lancet is used to scratch the skin under each drop. This allows the allergen to penetrate the skin. A different lancet is used for each allergen in order to avoid cross-contamination. Because the lancets are tiny and merely scrape the skin without drawing blood, the procedure is not painful.

The allergens are left on the patient's skin for fifteen to thirty minutes. Then the health-care professional examines the patient's skin. If the patient is sensitive to a particular allergen, the skin where the allergen was applied will become red, irritated, and swollen, forming a red, itchy bump called a wheal. This indicates that the body is producing IgE in response to the allergen. And because the larger the wheal, the stronger the reaction, the test not only identifies an individual's allergy triggers but also the approximate level of sensitivity to a particular allergen. For this reason, the wheals are measured.

> I vividly recall my trip to the allergist's office to get my skin scratch test. I was a young child," says Weaver. "I had to lie face down while tiny needle sticks were applied in a grid-like fashion all over my back. To my surprise, the scratches did not hurt at all, but they did cause my back to feel very itchy. I was of course not able to scratch the testing area, so my mom had to fan my back to appease the itchy feeling. The experience lasted no more than 30 minutes.... Mom got a whole stack of information about my newly discovered allergies. We found out that not only was I allergic to shellfish, I also had multiple other food allergies including milk. Add to that my sensitivity to mold, dust mites, pets and pollen and, needless to say, we were overwhelmed. But, it was a great place to start us on the path to helping me feel better.[23]

Reactions to skin tests usually clear quickly. But since allergens are applied directly to an individual's skin, in cases of severe allergies, reactions can prove dangerous. One in one thousand allergy skin tests causes anaphylaxis. That is why the tests are always administered in a medical setting under the care of a trained professional who can administer emergency treatment if necessary. In fact, if a severe allergy is suspected, instead of skin testing, patients may be administered a radioallergosorbent test (RAST). This is a test in which a sample of the patient's blood is sent to a laboratory, where a health-care professional measures the number of IgE antibodies to specific allergens in the blood sample.

Pollen Counts

Newspapers and television news programs often report pollen counts. A pollen count measures the total number of grains of a particular pollen found in a cubic meter of air in a given day. The number is then given one of five ratings ranging from absent to very high.

The lowest rating is absent. As the name implies, there are no grains of pollen per cubic meter that day. A low rating counts one to ten grains per cubic meter. A moderate rating counts eleven ten to fifty. A high count is fifty-one to five hundred, and a very high count is more than five hundred grains per cubic meter.

The severity of an allergy sufferer's symptoms goes up with the rating. At absent and low, most people are untroubled. For sensitive people, symptoms start to appear at moderate. When the rating is high or very high, almost all individuals allergic to that particular pollen develop symptoms.

Windy weather usually increases pollen counts, while rain can temporarily wash pollen out of the air.

Food Challenge Test

Although both an allergy skin test and a RAST are fairly reliable, neither test is accurate 100 percent of the time. For a number of reasons, including the fact that these tests do not expose patients to allergens in the same manner as in real life, individuals may not react the same way as they do when they encounter the allergen in the environment. For unknown reasons, this is especially true when it comes to foods. That is why if a patient responds positively to a food in a skin or RAST test, many physicians administer a food challenge test.

In a controlled setting, where emergency medical care is available, patients are given increasingly larger doses of a suspected food. The first dose of the food is tiny. The amount is gradually increased at half-hour intervals until a reaction occurs or the patient consumes a normal amount of the food without reacting. Not only does the test establish exactly what foods a person is allergic to, it also accurately pinpoints the individual's degree of sensitivity to the food. This is especially important in food allergies. Dr. Charles Atkins of Denver's National Jewish Medical and Research Center explains:

> Some patients or their families become concerned that exposure to even tiny amounts of a food can cause a life-threatening reaction. These concerns occasionally interfere with participation in normal activities and can lead to social isolation. Although some patients are indeed exquisitely sensitive, others find that more of the food than was expected can be tolerated without a severe reaction – even though large positive skin tests and history suggest otherwise. This can be a relief for patients who have avoided activities out of concern about the possibility of exquisite sensitivity. Alternatively, some patients are found to be more sensitive than was previously expected. In this case, the importance of strict avoidance, as well as being thoroughly prepared to treat severe reactions, is enforced.[24]

Allergy Medications

Once allergy triggers are identified, patients are advised to avoid contact with the offending allergen whenever possible. If the body is not exposed to the allergen, the immune system will not overreact. Depending on the allergy trigger, this may or may not be reasonable. For instance, people allergic to penicillin can avoid the drug, as can people allergic to peanuts. Indeed, avoidance is the primary way people with drug or food allergies protect themselves against allergic reactions. Avoiding contact with pollen, dust mites, or mold is not as simple. Nor is it feasible for people with multiple allergies to avoid every allergen they react to. In cases when avoidance is not an

A variety of medicines are available to help people cope with their allergies.

option, medications that treat allergy symptoms are administered. These include antihistamines, decongestants, eye drops, and nasal sprays, and are most suitable for treating allergies that cause congestion and itching.

Antihistamines are the most common class of drugs used to treat allergies. Usually taken by mouth, antihistamines block the release of histamine, thus inhibiting an allergic reaction. According to Mindell,

> Histamine works by attaching itself to special sites on cells called receptors. Think of the receptor as a lock and histamine as the key. Histamine unlocks the receptor to begin the allergic cascade that causes allergic symptoms. Antihistamines attach themselves to the same receptors on cells as histamine, which prevents histamine from binding to these sites, thus dampening the allergic response.[25]

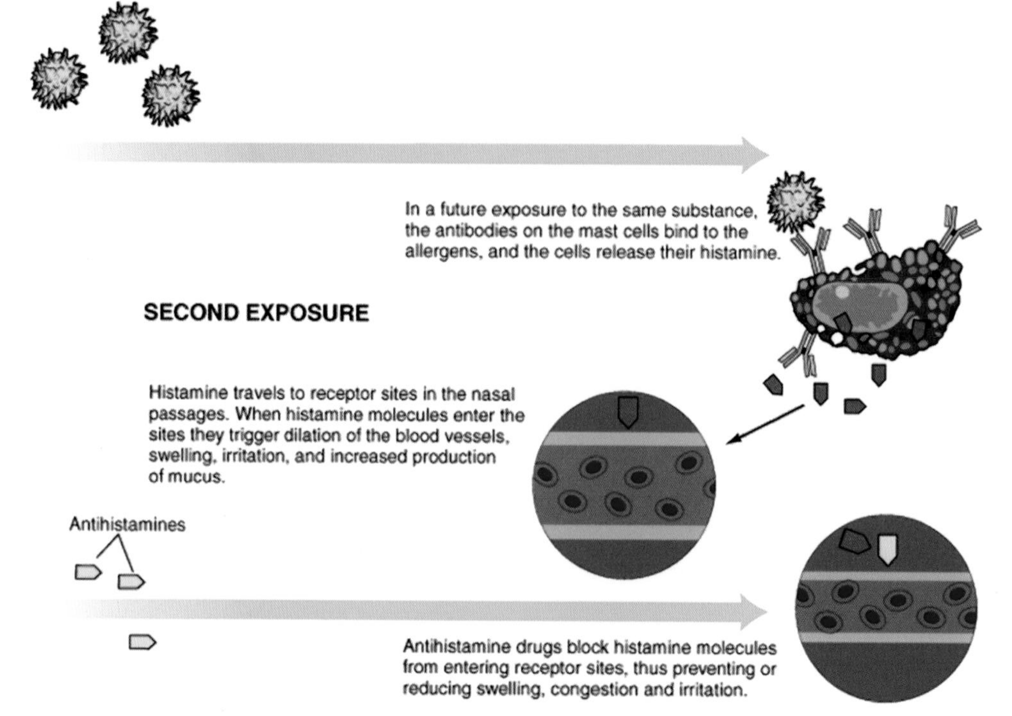

Antihistamines are fast acting, but their effect is short-lived. During allergy season, many individuals take one or more doses every day. And although they do inhibit unpleasant allergy symptoms such as itching, swelling, and sneezing, they do not stop them entirely. In addition, many antihistamines cause drowsiness and dizziness. They can also cause urinary tract blockages in men with enlarged prostate glands as well as blockages in the lungs of people with asthma.

Despite these health risks, antihistamines are important tools in treating allergies. Authors Kwong and Cook agree: "In spite of these cautions a medication like Benadryl [a popular antihistamine] remains a powerful and useful anti-allergy medication because it works fast and is quickly absorbed."[26]

Antihistamines can also be applied as a topical cream to relieve itchy rashes and in eye drops to counteract red, itchy eyes.

Decongestants and Other Treatments

Decongestants are another common allergy treatment. They relieve nasal congestion and blockages caused by hay fever and other inhaled allergies. Decongestants work by constricting blood vessels in nasal passages, which reverses the swelling that causes nasal congestion. Decongestants are taken orally. Their side effects are the opposite of those of antihistamines, causing nervousness, rapid heart rate, and insomnia. They also elevate blood pressure, which can be dangerous for people who have high blood pressure or heart disease.

To lessen the side effects of decongestants and antihistamines, some allergy medications combine the two drugs. Such combinations relieve itching, swelling, sneezing, and congestion without causing drowsiness or nervousness. These medications are available over the counter and in stronger, prescription formulas.

Decongestants are common allergy treatments.

Nasal corticosteroids are another way to treat allergic rhinitis. This medication, administered as a nasal spray, contains steroids, man-made copies of inflammation- fighting hormones found in the human body. When the medication is sprayed into the nostrils, it delivers a powerful dose of an anti-inflammatory medication directly to the nasal passages. The medication blocks the inflammatory process, relieving sneezing, nasal discharge, swelling, and congestion. Because it is sprayed directly into the nose, rather than ingested, it does not cause the side effects, such as sleeplessness, indigestion, or dizziness, commonly associated with oral steroid medications, which are sometimes used to treat allergic reactions to drugs. However, nasal corticosteroids can cause a burning sensation in the nose, and they do not produce instant results. Patients must use the medication for several days before seeing a marked improvement in their condition. Full effectiveness can take two to three weeks of daily use. That is why nasal sprays are often combined with antihistamines or decongestants and why many patients with seasonal allergies start using a nasal spray before the allergy season begins. According to Kwong and Cook, "Nasal steroids work well if they are used prior to anticipated seasonal allergic rhinitis. This is certainly something to keep in mind."[27]

Immunotherapy

Immunotherapy, or allergy shots, is another treatment option. In immunotherapy, small amounts of whatever substances an individual is allergic to are injected under the individual's skin. At first, the injected substance is highly diluted so that it does not cause an allergic reaction. Each succeeding injection contains a slightly higher dose of the allergen. The goal is to gradually desensitize the immune system to the allergen so that it no longer reacts when it is exposed to the substance. According to the American Academy of Allergy, Asthma, and Immunology,

> Allergen immunotherapy works like a vaccine. Your body responds to the injected amount of a particular allergen, given in gradually increasing doses, by developing

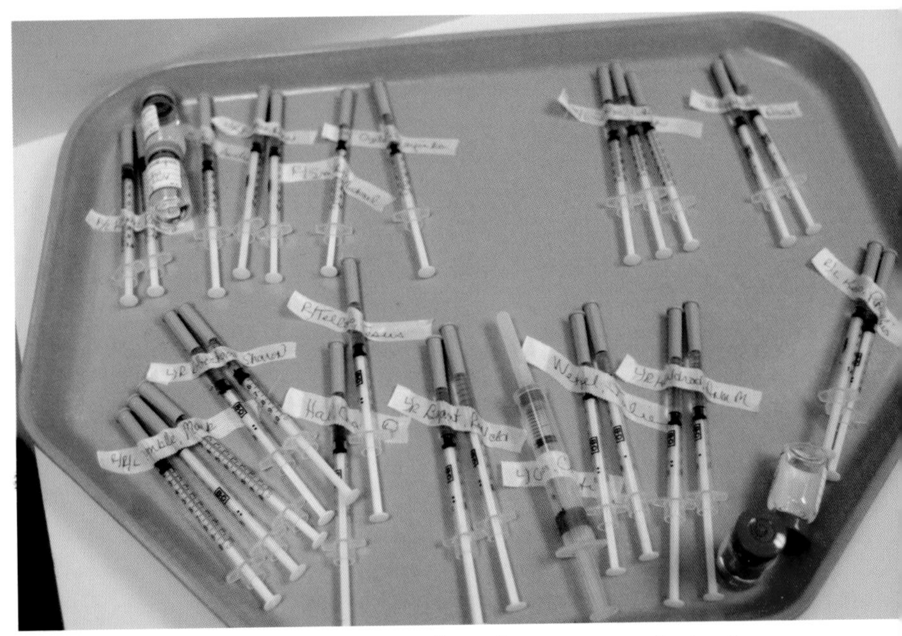

A tray holds allergy immunotherapy shots for sixteen patients at the Hershey, Pennsylvania Medical Center. Shots like these can help someone become desensitized to an allergen so they no longer react to it.

an immunity or tolerance to the allergen(s). As a result of these immune changes, immunotherapy can lead to decreased, minimal, or no allergy symptoms when you are exposed to the allergen(s) included in the vaccine.[28]

Immunotherapy is usually administered once or twice a week for three to six months. This is known as the build-up phase in which the dosage keeps being increased. Once an effective dose is reached, individuals are administered allergy shots once every two to four weeks. This is known as the maintenance phase and, depending on the patient, continues from three to five years or longer. The amount of the maintenance dose is determined by the severity of the patient's allergies as measured by the size of the wheals in the allergy skin test.

Because thin, small needles are used, immunotherapy is not painful. The shot site can burn and itch, however. The therapy,

A Universal Problem

Allergies are a global health problem. Tests and surveys of population samples throughout the world indicate large numbers of people already have allergies or are at risk for developing them. For instance, the results of skin tests in Hong Kong indicate that half of all the children there are sensitive to allergens, particularly dust mites and cockroaches. Other cities in China report similar results. Tests in Costa Rica of school-age children show one-fourth to be vulnerable.

German tests indicate that one-third of all Germans are sensitive to pollens and dust mites, while surveys show that one-quarter of the population there have current allergies. Tests in Mumbai (formerly called Bombay), India, indicate that one-fifth of the population in that city are sensitive to dust mites, while studies in Kuwait show that one-quarter of Kuwaitis are also sensitive to dust mites.

which helps 80 percent of those treated, provides relief for people for whom allergy medications prove to be ineffective. This includes individuals with severe inhalant allergies, those with year-round allergies who do not want to take allergy medicine every day, and those who want to avoid the unpleasant side effects caused by allergy medication. Results, however, are not immediate. It can take a year before patients notice a significant improvement. And, because exposure to even minute quantities of an allergen can be life threatening to some people with food or drug allergies, immunotherapy is not used to treat these individuals, although scientists are working on the possibility. Despite these drawbacks, many people find relief through immunotherapy. Sarah, who gets a shot in each arm every other week, explains: "Before I started, I was getting sick all the time. You get to a point when you don't want to live like that. I've been on the shots for a year now and have only been sick once. The shots help a lot. It's worth it." [29]

Treating Anaphylaxis

The only treatment for people with food and drug allergies is avoidance. If these individuals, as well as other individuals with severe allergies, develop anaphylaxis, urgent treatment is required. Because anaphylaxis can cause shock in less than an hour, it is considered a medical emergency.

Anaphylaxis is treated with antihistamines and epinephrine. Epinephrine is a chemical that narrows blood vessels and causes airway muscles to relax. This causes an individual's blood pressure to rise and relieves breathing problems. In cases of anaphylaxis, quick use of this medication can be life saving.

Epinephrine is administered via injection. Most individuals with a history of life-threatening food or insect venom allergies carry at least one EpiPen with them at all times. It is a

Jack, pictured with his mother, Allison Bloomfield, has a severe peanut allergy and could die if exposed to them. The EpiPen Allison is holding can provide emergency relief to Jack and is always kept nearby.

self-injectable dose of epinephrine in the form of a syringe-like device.

A dose is administered by plunging the EpiPen into the fleshy part of the thigh. In extremely severe cases more than one dose may be administered. According to the CBS network's medical correspondent, Emily Senjay, MD, the pen is not difficult to use. "Take it out of the plastic coating, pop off the gray protective top, and put it right into the thigh with force. You want to leave it there for about five to ten seconds, pull it out, [and it] saves your life."[30]

A dose lasts no more than twenty minutes, which usually gives individuals enough time to get to a medical facility, where treatment can be administered. Canadian Olympic runner LaDonna Antoine-Watkins recalls her experience: "I was eating a meal with my teammates when I started feeling unwell. My throat was closing up and I knew I was in trouble.... My coach stayed calm and drove me to the hospital. And once I'd had the epinephrine auto-injector, I knew that I was going to be all right."[31]

Allergies can cause a number of problems. Once allergy triggers are identified, patients can prevent an allergic reaction by avoiding triggering allergens. When this is not feasible, a wide range of different treatments provide relief and, in some cases, save lives. Indeed, according to experts at the Allergy Authority, a Web site dedicated to educating the public about allergies, "With more awareness about [allergies] these days and many treatments available, allergy sufferers can find relief from their symptoms so they can enjoy every day all year long."[32]

CHAPTER THREE

Alternative and Complementary Treatments

Although traditional allergy treatments can be effective, some individuals turn to other forms of treatment. They do this for a number of reasons. One reason is that allergy medications can cause unpleasant side effects that impact a patient's quality of life. And because they are short-acting and require multiple doses over an extended period of time, many people look for ways to reduce their dosages.

Immunotherapy, too, has drawbacks. It can take a year to be effective, does not work for everyone, and is costly and time consuming. Also, some individuals are uncomfortable with shots. "I discovered how hard it would be to get my shots, even with good intentions," explains Penny, who found allergy shots too time consuming. "For one thing, I could not find a doctor who could see me beyond normal business hours so I struggled to take off time during the workday. Once I found a doctor I liked, he was so busy that I often had trouble finding an appointment time with him that fit my allergy shot schedule."[33]

For these and other reasons, many individuals turn to alternative treatments. As with conventional therapies, the goal is to minimize allergy symptoms; however, despite the fact that alternative treatments are considered to be gentler and more

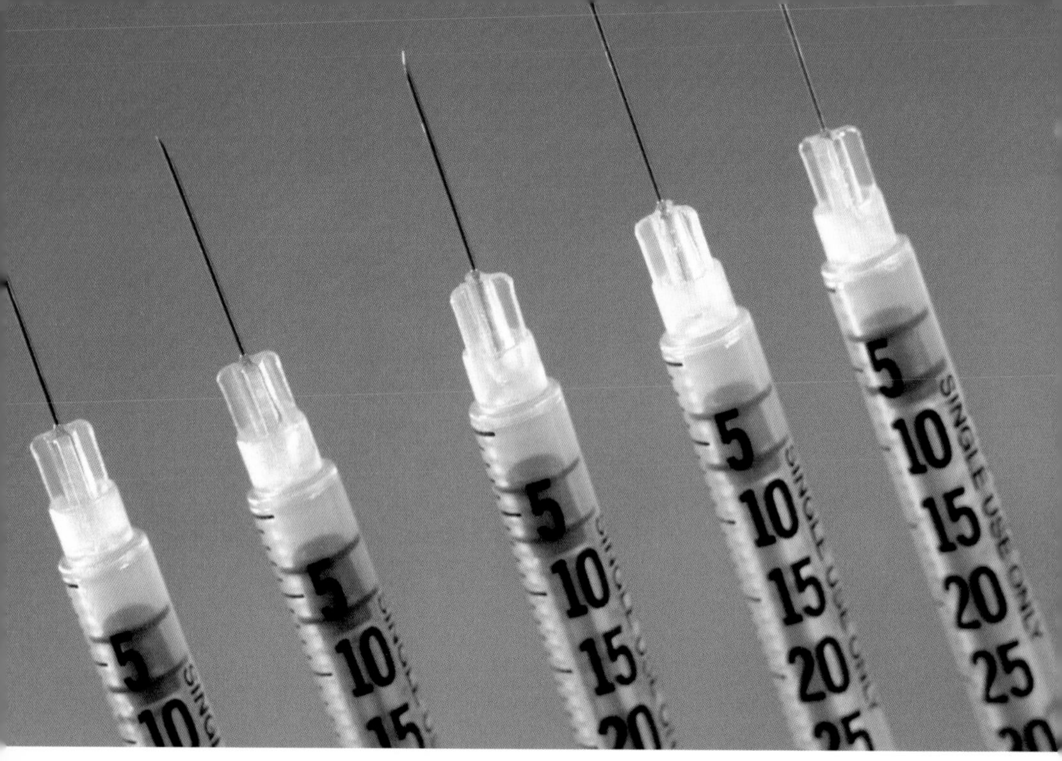

Some allergy sufferers find the many shots involved in immunotherapy difficult to deal with, and look for alternative treatments.

natural than traditional medical treatments, they too are not without risk.

What Are Alternative and Complementary Treatments?

Alternative treatments are treatments that are not widely accepted by the traditional medical community in the United States. Unlike conventional treatments, alternative treatments are not subjected to strict testing by the federal Food and Drug Administration (FDA), a government agency that sets standards for the safe use of drugs. Many alternative treatments undergo limited testing and therefore lack enough information to show clearly whether the treatment is safe or effective. Moreover, although many alternative health-care practitioners go through intensive training, some do not. Some alternative practitioners are not required to undergo years of schooling or take comprehensive licensing exams, as do medical doctors.

Despite the lack of regulation and testing, many traditional health-care professionals believe that alternative treatments can be beneficial in treating allergies, especially when they are

Allergies and Ancient History

People have suffered with allergies for thousands of years. In 2700 B.C. ancient Chinese doctors wrote about using an herb called ephedra to treat plant fever, a term that medical historians say was used to describe hay fever, or seasonal pollen allergies. Interestingly, a drug called ephedrine, which is derived from ephedra, is used in modern decongestants.

Across the world in ancient Egypt, the early Egyptian pharaoh Menses is believed to have died from anaphylaxis caused by a wasp sting. Inscriptions about wasps are found throughout his tomb. His may be the first recorded death due to an insect sting.

Years later, in about 400 B.C., the first case of food allergies was recorded. The ancient Greek doctor Hippocrates reported a case of illness caused by a bad reaction to cheese. From the description, medical historians believe Hippocrates was reporting a food allergy.

In ancient times, ephedra was used to treat plant fever, referred to today as hay fever or seasonal pollen allergies.

combined with conventional allergy treatments in a method known as complementary treatments. Such treatments may reduce inflammation, protect patients against secondary infections, and improve a patient's general health and well-being. As a result, individuals gain more control over their allergies. Geoffrey, a family doctor who incorporates complementary treatment in his medical practice, explains: "I think of it in terms of having more tools at our disposal – being able to tackle things from a different angle when standard medicine isn't hitting the spot."[34] Herbal remedies, aromatherapy, nutritional supplements, and acupuncture are among the most popular alternative treatments for allergies.

Herbal Treatments

Herbal treatment is an ancient form of medical treatment, dating back thousands of years. It uses the stems, roots, leaves, bark, and seeds of plants known to have healing properties to treat any number of illnesses. In fact, at least 25 percent of all traditional medications are derived from plant sources or contain chemicals that imitate plant compounds. Herbs used to

Butterbur grows in the wild in Japan. Butterbur contains natural substances that may help relieve the inflammation caused by allergies.

treat allergies contain substances that appear to reduce inflammation. Users say they have a similar effect as antihistamines, relieving nasal congestion, sneezing, and itching.

There are a number of herbs with anti-inflammatory properties. These include garlic, ginger, ginkgo, turmeric, lungwort, licorice, milk thistle, and sarsaparilla, to name a few. These herbs are taken in capsule form or as a tea, either alone or in combination.

Two herbs in particular, butterbur and nettles, have aroused growing interest in the treatment of allergies. Both have been the subjects of recent studies. Butterbur is a shrub that grows in North America, Europe, and Asia. It has been used to treat asthma, coughs, and headaches for many years. Butterbur contains petasins, natural substances that relieve inflammation and relax the smooth muscles in the airways. A 2005 study in Landquart, Switzerland, compared the effect of butterbur extract to equal doses of a traditional antihistamine in 330 patients with nasal allergy symptoms. The researchers found that both treatments provided equal allergy relief. Another study in 2006 in Romanshorn, Switzerland, yielded similar results. In that study 90 percent of the 580 subjects treated with butterbur reported a significant improvement in their symptoms. According to researcher Andres Schapowal, "Butterbur … is an effective treatment for intermittent allergic rhinitis symptoms and is well tolerated. The effects of this herbal medicine are clear."[35]

Nettles, too, appear to calm inflammation. Leaves from the herb have been used to treat inflammation as far back as ancient Greece. A 1990 study conducted at the National College of Naturopathic Medicine in Portland, Oregon, compared the effect of nettles on 69 individuals with hay fever to that of a placebo, or fake remedy. After one week, 58 percent of the subjects taking nettles reported improvement in their symptoms compared with 37 percent of the placebo group. A few other small studies have produced similar results. But the herb has not been studied enough for researchers to be able to explain how nettles calm inflammation or to confirm if the herb is indeed effective. Still, many allergy sufferers say that nettles ease their symptoms. Among them is Andrew Weil, MD, the director of the Program in Integrative Medicine at the University of Arizona College of Medicine in Tucson: "I've found that this herb relieved hay fever symptoms. Use a freeze-dried extract of the leaves, which is sold in capsules and is widely available in health food stores. Take one or two capsules every 2 to 4 hours as needed."[36]

Aromatherapy

Still another herb, eucalyptus, is another ancient treatment for upper respiratory congestion. But rather than ingesting the herb, patients inhale oil extracted from the plant. According to Eucalyptus Nurseries, a grower and supplier of eucalyptus,

> Inhaling eucalyptus oil coats the respiratory tract forming a protective layer with the effects being almost immediate. The eucalyptus oil expands alveoli (tiny air sacs in the lungs), which increases airflow into the lungs and increases oxygen flow to the body, temporarily expanding lung capacity. Eucalyptus helps to thin the mucus in the nasal passages and lungs, which … inhibits growth of bacteria and viral replication, reducing the likelihood of colds and related infections.[37]

Inhaling oils derived from a plant to treat an illness is known as aromatherapy. In aromatherapy, oil is usually placed in a special diffuser. There, it heats up and disperses into the air as a mist. Patients inhale the mist into their bloodstream through the lungs. The oil can also be dispersed via a steam vaporizer or placed in a large pot of steaming water. Patients lean over the pot and, using a towel to make a tent over their head, breathe in the scented steam. Although there is no definitive proof that aromatherapy is truly effective, many individuals find the therapy soothing. According to Mindell, treating nasal congestion in this manner "helps clear out your airways and relieves congestion without drying out your sinuses, as decongestants

A vial of eucalyptus oil. Eucalyptus can help relieve upper respiratory congestion.

often do." Such treatment, he explains, is "old fashioned, but very effective."[38]

Nutritional Supplements and Diet

While some individuals turn to herbs, others find that complementing traditional allergy treatment with nutritional supplements lessens their symptoms. Vitamins B, C, and E are among the most popular of these supplements. These vitamins are antioxidants, natural substances that help protect the body against damage caused by oxidation, a process in which cells are weakened when they come in contact with oxygen molecules. Cell damage can aggravate allergy symptoms and make the body less able to fight off secondary infections.

Besides being antioxidants, these vitamins have other helpful properties. For instance, all three vitamins appear to have anti-inflammatory qualities. Moreover, vitamin E may reduce the production of IgE antibodies. Indeed, some scientists theorize that low levels of vitamin E make people more susceptible to allergies. A 2001 study at Aberdeen University in Scotland found that infants born to women who had a diet rich in vitamin E were less sensitive to allergens than those whose mothers consumed less vitamin E. The scientists determined this by performing a RAST test on blood taken from the infant's umbilical cords. According to scientist John Harvey, MD, "This is the first study world-wide to have shown an effect of maternal diet

A model displays bottles of the Japanese soft drink Arelsmooth. The manufacturer claims the drink can help protect against allergies because it contains 100mg of flavonoids, a type of chemical believed to have many beneficial effects.

during pregnancy on evidence of allergy in the newborn."[39] A second study that monitors the babies to see if vitamin E has a long-term effect on allergy prevention is currently under way.

Since consuming all three vitamins is an important part of maintaining a healthy diet, whether or not these nutrients have anti-inflammatory properties, it cannot hurt individuals with allergies to add more foods rich in these nutrients to their diet. Good sources of vitamin E include leafy green vegetables and nuts. Vitamin C is found in citrus fruit, berries, peppers, and broccoli. Whole grains, vegetables, eggs, dairy products, meats, and fish are all good sources of vitamin B.

In addition, many alternative health-care practitioners suggest that people with allergies add a number of other foods to their diet, such as salmon, cod, tuna, olive oil, nuts, flaxseed, and wheat germ. These foods are rich in omega-3 fatty acids, which appear to naturally inhibit the release of histamines.

Brightly colored fruits and vegetables of all types are also recommended. They contain flavonoids, a group of more than four thousand substances that are believed to have many health benefits, including anti-inflammatory, antihistamine, and antioxidant properties. According to Mindell,

> For allergy sufferers flavonoids can be a godsend. First, they strengthen small blood vessels called capillaries, which help protect cells from foreign particles (such as allergies) by forming a protective barrier. Second, flavonoids reduce inflammation typical of allergies and help normalize immune function, which reduces allergy symptoms. In particular, flavonoids help stabilize mast cells, the immune cells that produce histamines when they encounter allergens. Flavonoids calm down these overexcited cells, preventing the release of histamine, which is responsible for those annoying allergy symptoms. Last but not least, by maintaining optimal antioxidant levels in the body, flavonoids help the body cleanse itself of pollution, toxins, and other chemicals that can send the immune system into overdrive and trigger an allergic reaction.[40]

One flavonoid in particular, quercetin, has been the subject of allergy studies. Found in apples, onions, berries, grapes, red wine, and green tea, it is chemically similar to a drug used in allergy and asthma medications. Alternative practitioners say that quercetin is a powerful antihistamine that also enhances lung health. A University of Nottingham, England, study examined this theory. In the study, which lasted from 1991 to 2000, the lung functions of 2,633 adults who ate at least five apples per week were compared with those who ate fewer apples. The researchers found that those subjects who ate the most apples had significantly better lung function than the other subjects. This means they could exhale air more easily, had less coughing and congestion and less severe upper respiratory allergy and asthma symptoms. Another 2000 British study at St. George's Hospital in London yielded similar results. Commenting on these studies, Dianne Hyson, a nutrition researcher with the University of California–Davis Medical Center, says, "This research adds to the growing body of science demonstrating that eating apples may improve health including lung function."[41]

Acupuncture and Allergies

Acupuncture is another alternative treatment that some allergy sufferers find beneficial. It is an ancient form of Chinese medicine based on the theory that healthy people have an energy called qi (pronounced "chi") flowing through their bodies. If qi is blocked, the immune system over- or underreacts, and illnesses and inflammation occur.

Acupuncture involves the insertion of hair-thin needles into specific points in the body where acupuncturists say energy channels are blocked. The insertion of the needles is supposed to open up the channels, allowing the qi to flow freely. Since the needles are extremely thin, this procedure is not painful.

Acupuncturists say that once the channel is unblocked, the immune system will return to normal and inflammation will be reduced. Even though many people say that acupuncture treatments have improved their health, there is little evidence

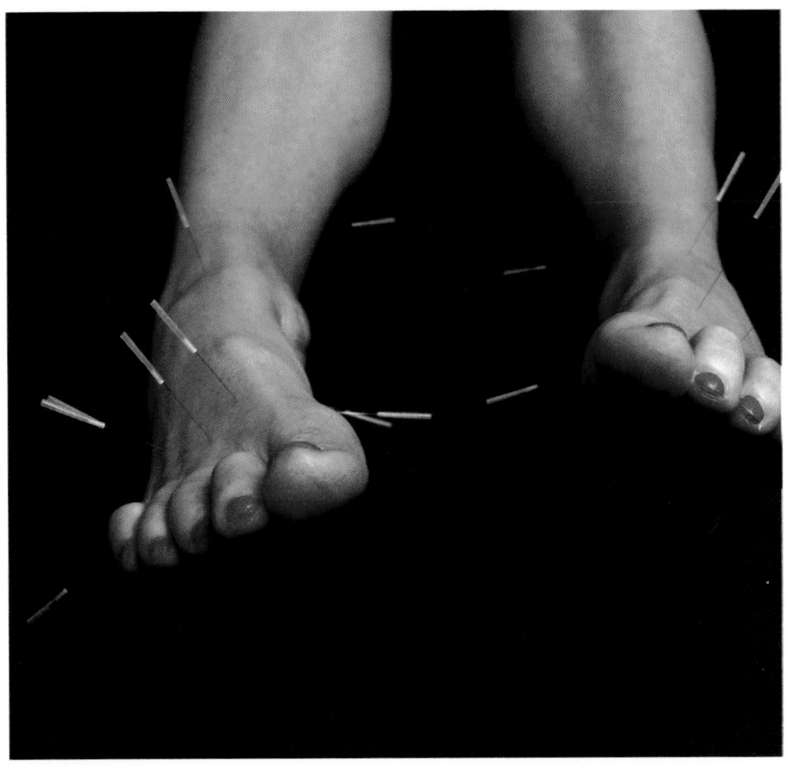

Acupuncture treatment is applied to a woman's feet. Acupuncture is an ancient form of traditional Chinese medicine that may help to relieve allergies.

in Western science to prove that qi exists. Nor have there been many studies on the effectiveness of acupuncture in treating allergies. One of the few is a 2004 study conducted in a Hong Kong allergy clinic that yielded promising results. In this study, children with seasonal allergies were divided into two groups. The first group was treated with acupuncture to relieve their allergy symptoms. The second group was treated with what appeared to be acupuncture. In reality, the needles were not inserted deeply enough to be effective. So, the second group unknowingly acted as a control group, receiving no actual treatment. The real and fake treatments were administered twice a week for eight weeks. The subjects' symptoms were checked daily and scored on a numerical scale. The subjects treated

About Asthma

Many people with allergies develop asthma. It is a disorder of the respiratory system that affects the lungs and thus an individual's ability to breathe. When a person breathes, oxygen travels in and carbon dioxide out of the body through airways. This is a roadlike network that goes from the nose and mouth through the windpipe to the lungs. Normally, if an irritant such as dust, smoke, or pollen is inhaled, the lining of the airways becomes swollen and inflamed. Mucus, a sticky substance that traps the irritant is produced. A cough expels the irritant-containing mucus from the body. This is the body's way of protecting the lungs.

When people with asthma inhale an irritant, the lungs overreact, much like an allergic reaction. Unchecked inflammation causes the swollen airways to narrow, while the production of excess mucus forms sticky plugs that block the narrow airways. At the same time, the smooth muscles that surround the airways constrict and squeeze the airways. As a result, it becomes increasingly difficult for the individual to breathe. Usually the lungs of people with asthma react this way because they are allergic to the irritant that triggered the response.

with acupuncture had lower scores, which translated to fewer allergy symptoms during the treatment period. Moreover, they continued to have fewer allergy symptoms for ten weeks thereafter. The researchers concluded that "active acupuncture was more effective than sham acupuncture in decreasing the symptom scores for persistent allergic rhinitis and increasing the symptom-free days."[42] Scientists hope to do a large-scale study in the future to try to verify the results of this study.

Meanwhile, supplementing traditional allergy treatment with acupuncture therapy may help people with allergies. But it is important to make sure the acupuncturist is a trained professional. Poorly inserted needles can cause pain and bruising, and unclean needles can lead to infection.

Are Alternative Treatments Safe?

Just as acupuncture administered by an untrained practitioner can cause health issues, other alternative treatments can also cause problems. Herbs, for example, whether ingested or dispersed via aromatherapy, are powerful substances, which, like traditional medications, can cause side effects. Author Linda Gamlin explains:

> Herbs produce side effects in just the same way as medicinal drugs do. This is almost inevitable—anything that alters body functions enough to act as a drug will usually have some unwanted effects. In the case of herbal medicines, there is an added complication. Plants contain dozens, even hundreds, of different chemical substances, many of which have no benefits to humans at all—they are just plain toxic. These plant toxins can produce various unpleasant side effects on their own, to add to the side effects of the useful ingredients. So the possibility of side effects is actually higher with herbal medicines than with medicinal drugs.[43]

Like many natural substances, nettle leaves can have both beneficial and harmful effects and must be used with care.

Nettles, for instance, can cause nausea and an upset stomach. Pregnant women should never take this herb, since it may cause birth defects in a fetus. In addition, it can worsen heart and kidney problems in people with diseases of these organs.

Butterbur also is not without risk. It can cause headache, fatigue, dizziness, and stomach upset. Moreover, butterbur contains toxic chemicals that, if they are not removed before the herb is ingested, can cause kidney and liver damage and may cause cancer. And, since the U.S. government does not regulate the purity of herbal substances, it is possible, though unlikely, for butterbur that contains toxins to be sold.

Further complicating matters is that, in the absence of governmental regulations, unknown ingredients may be added to an herbal remedy. According to the National Center for Environmental Health, some herbal products do not contain the ingredients listed on the label. Still others contain the very drugs individuals are trying to avoid. An example is an herbal

Alternative Remedies for Allergies

Type of Treatment	Description of Treatment	How it works
Herbal	Ingestion or topical application of stems, roots, leaves, bark and seeds of plants known to have healing properties.	Reduces inflammation, similar to antihistamines.
Aromatherapy	Inhalation of plant essential oils in a steam vaporizer, electric diffuser, or pot of steaming water.	Relieves congestion, increases oxygen-flow to lungs and reduces mucus, helps in relaxation.
Nutritional supplements and dietary changes	Use of vitamins and/or foods with large quantities of omega-3 fatty acids (like salmon and olive oil), flavonoids (like apples), and antioxidants.	Vitamins B, C, E are antioxidants and have anti-inflammatory properties. The flavonoid quercetin is a powerful antihistamine.
Acupuncture	Use of hair-thin needles placed into specific points in the body, which allows "chi" (energy) blocks to be eliminated.	Reduction of inflammation and pain.

skin cream that was sold in Great Britain and that was used to treat allergic dermatitis. The cream contained a powerful steroid drug that produces a number of serious side effects, especially in children, the group the cream's producers targeted.

Lack of regulations and monitoring also means that there is no set dosage for herbal products. Consequently, herbal treatments may be weaker or stronger than patients anticipate. In fact, there have been cases in which herbal treatments have been found to be three times the strength written on the label. This is troubling because some herbs contain substances that are helpful in small amounts but can be poisonous in large doses.

Moreover, since herbs are plants, they can cause an allergic reaction in individuals with pollen allergies. Butterbur, for instance, is chemically similar to ragweed, a common allergy trigger. Inhaling essential oils via aromatherapy can also trigger an allergic reaction. Powerful scents can irritate the airways of sensitive individuals, causing nasal congestion and even an asthma attack. Even herbal creams can cause trouble. Some contain royal jelly, a substance taken from bees. Such creams can cause anaphylaxis in susceptible individuals.

Nutritional supplements, too, are not without risk. Large doses of vitamin C and E can cause problems like stomach upset, diarrhea, and nausea. High doses of vitamin B3 can cause itchy red skin, while high doses of vitamin B12 can cause an acnelike condition to develop. High doses of vitamin B6 can be even more dangerous, causing numbness and tingling in a person's hands and feet and difficulty walking. More troubling, many nutritional supplements contain additives and fillers such as soy oil or cornstarch. If individuals allergic to these substances unknowingly ingest them in a vitamin pill the results can be devastating. Mindell explains:

> You can't be allergic to vitamins, because you could not survive without them, but it's possible to be allergic to the soy oil used in your vitamin pill or the cornstarch or the dairy by-products used as fillers and binders. There-

> fore, you must read the label carefully before buying any products. Look for products that do not contain artificial flavoring, and if you are allergic to either corn, soy, dairy, yeast, wheat, or gluten, be sure to buy products that specifically state that they do not contain these ingredients. If you are in doubt, call the manufacturer to make sure. If you are highly allergic to a substance, even a small amount of it can trigger symptoms.[44]

Clearly alternative treatments can pose health risks. Yet many people with allergies say that these treatments help relieve allergy symptoms and enhance their general health. For these individuals, the improvement in the quality of their lives is worth the risk.

CHAPTER FOUR

Living with Allergies

Living with allergies is not easy. Individuals must cope with unpleasant symptoms that make them feel ill and can lead to secondary infections or asthma attacks. Those with severe allergies live with the threat of anaphylaxis. Such problems can make individuals feel that they have lost control over their lives. By acting defensively and making changes in their lives that reduce the possibility of an allergic reaction occurring, allergy sufferers regain control. Sam, a lifelong allergy sufferer, puts it this way: "Sometimes I wish I did not have allergies, but I know that is not realistic. I doubt my allergies will ever go away, but I'm glad that there are ways to control them.... I just do whatever I can to feel better."[45]

Allergy-Proofing the Home

Allergy-proofing the home is one way that people with allergies cope. A wide variety of allergens are found in a typical home. These include dust mites, mold, cockroach droppings, and various chemicals. By eliminating or at least reducing their exposure to such substances, even people with multiple allergies can significantly reduce their allergy symptoms. Dr. Pamela A. Georgeson, president of Kenwood Allergy and Asthma Center in Chesterfield Township, Michigan, explains: "When you have indoor allergies, you'll wake up, feel miserable, tired, and your eyes water all the time. It really impacts the quality of life. You don't have to go to extremes, though, to make changes in the home that allow you to live a normal life."[46]

One way to combat allergies is to keep the inside of the home as free of dust and other allergens as possible, by dusting and vacuuming frequently.

There are many steps individuals can take to reduce allergens in their homes, and there are many products on the market that help clean indoor air. For instance, using an air purifier with a high efficiency particle air (HEPA) filter, which traps allergens, can remove more than 90 percent of allergens from the air. Such a device is especially effective in the bedroom, where dust mites are commonly found. Experts estimate that the average bed contains more than 2 million dust mites. According to Dr. Heidi Zafra of Philadelphia's St. Christopher's Hospital for Children, "When you shake your pillow and the dust flies, there's excrements from the dust mites, and that's what you inhale, and that's what irritates your nose and lungs."[47]

Covering pillows, mattresses, and box springs with a zippered microfiber cover that repels dust mites, reduces dust mites in beds. Washing bed linens in hot water once a week also destroys dust mites. New York University Medical Center's Dr. Morris Nejat explains:

> You want to get special covers to put on the mattress, the box spring and the pillowcases. What this does is, it encases these things, to keep the dust mite feces inside the mattress, and keep you from breathing them in while you're sleeping. Then you would wash all the bedding in hot water, over 130 degrees Fahrenheit, once a week. What that'll do is, that will kill and denature dust mites and their feces, so that they are no longer allergenic.[48]

Removing bed skirts, fabric headboards, and stuffed animals from the bed—all items that attract dust mites—also helps.

Vacuuming carpets and rugs everyday with a vacuum that uses a HEPA filter is another step individuals can take. The filter traps the allergens, which a traditional vaccum could otherwise stir up. Rugs and carpets, especially shag carpets, are prime spots for dust mites, pet dander, mold, and other allergens to accumulate. According to Mindell, "Wall-to-wall carpeting can mean wall-to-wall dust mites."[49]

In fact, some individuals remove all rugs and carpets entirely and replace them with smooth flooring such as vinyl, wood, or tile in order to completely dislodge dust mites and other allergens. That is what Sarah did. She explains: "I can't live in a bubble, but I try to keep my house as free of the things I am allergic to as I can. I noticed a big difference when I got rid of some of my carpet and put down tile floors. As soon as I can afford it, I plan to pick up the remaining carpet and replace it with wood floors."[50]

Besides vacuuming, frequent housecleaning is another way to reduce household allergens. Reducing clutter, such as piles of newspapers, books, or knick-knacks, reduces places for dust to accumulate. Housecleaning, however, can be problematic for sensitive people. Inhaling cleaning chemicals or dust can trigger an allergic reaction. To solve this problem, some individuals hire a professional housekeeper. Or, if this is not possible, they wear a protective mask that filters out allergens while they clean.

Other Household Actions

Using a dehumidifier to dry out household air is another way individuals can fight dust mites and mold, both of which thrive on moisture. Mold frequently grows in bathrooms, kitchens, laundry rooms, and damp basements. Running an exhaust fan in these rooms helps keep them dry, as does fixing leaky pipes, drying bath enclosures after bathing, and avoiding the use of bathroom rugs, which trap mold. Cleaning bathrooms at least once a week with a cleaning agent that contains bleach, which kills mold, is also highly effective.

The leaves and soil of indoor houseplants also accumulate mold. So do the needles of live Christmas trees, which can also cause problems for those allergic to pine needles. For this reason, many people with mold allergies get rid of houseplants and opt for an artificial Christmas tree. According to David Khan, associate professor of internal medicine at the University of Texas Southwestern Medical Center in Dallas, "Any live Christmas tree can cause allergies because anything from the

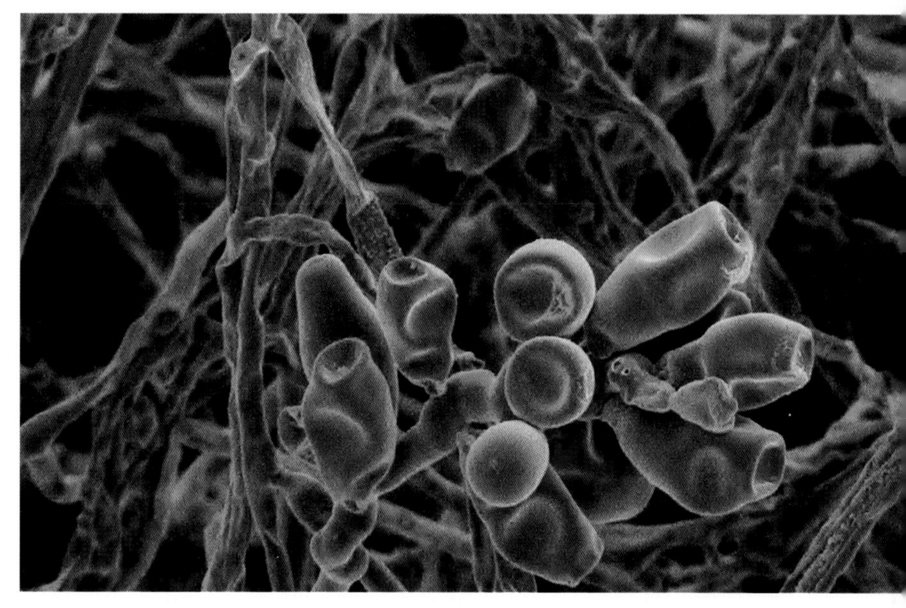

A magnified view of Drechlera, a mold that is common in household bathrooms and can be a cause of allergies.

outside that's brought inside is likely to bring mold spores with it.... All in all, getting an artificial tree and keeping it dust-free is probably the healthiest bet for an allergy sufferer."[51]

Cockroaches are another problematic indoor allergen. They can be found in any building, but are especially a problem in crowded urban areas where many people live in apartment buildings or row houses. Cracks in attached walls allow the insects to move between residences easily. According to the Asthma and Allergy Foundation of America, at least 78 percent of urban homes have cockroaches. Taking steps to keep an apartment or private home roach free lessens a person's exposure. Such steps include sealing cracks in the walls, not leaving food out, cleaning up crumbs, and using roach traps. Hiring an exterminator to destroy cockroaches in the home is another coping strategy. During the fumigation, and for several hours thereafter, some individuals stay out of their homes, since the chemicals used in the process can trigger an allergic reaction in sensitive individuals.

Pets and Allergies

Another common allergen found in many homes is pet dander. Although pets are beloved members of many households, pet dander can cause problems for susceptible individuals. As a result, although it is difficult, many allergy sufferers give up their pets. Or, when a pet dies, they do not get another one. "We had two cats," Alan, who is allergic to cat dander, explains. "Whenever I petted them, then touched my face, my eyes would blow up and water, and my nose would run. I didn't know what caused this. But after both the cats died and the symptoms stopped, I realized I was allergic to cats. I like cats and my wife loves them. Because of my allergy, we didn't get another cat. It was a major and difficult choice."[52]

Indeed, living without a pet is such a difficult decision that an estimated 75 percent of people advised by a physician to give up their pets do not do so. Instead, they take a number of steps to keep their allergies under control. Keeping pets outdoors

A highly magnified view of cat dander—the cause of human allergies to cats—on a piece of cat hair.

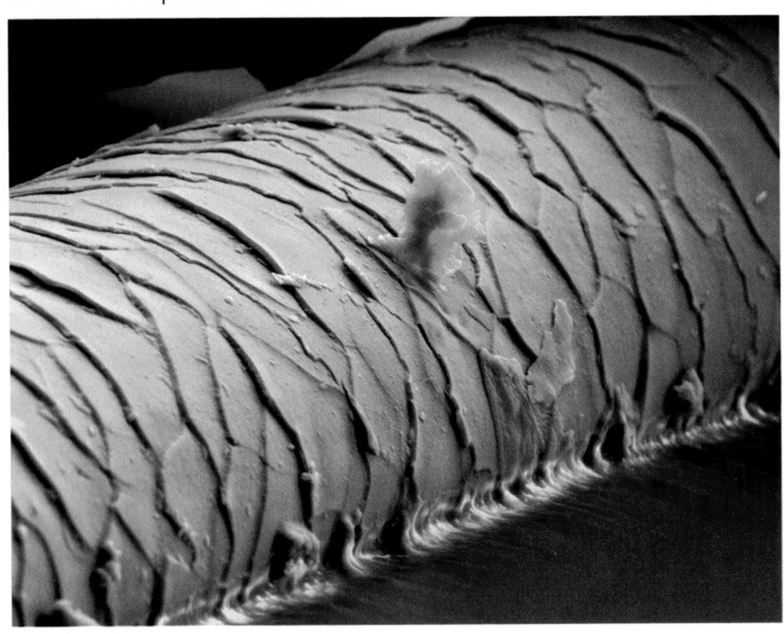

as much as possible is one measure. Kwong explains how this helped his allergic patient, B., whose wife refused to give up the family dog. "They ... built a nice kennel. The dog was ... restricted to a spacious section of the yard and not allowed into the house. B. was fine with this arrangement and his wife was happy."[53]

If pets are allowed in the house, keeping them off upholstered furniture, where pet dander settles, and out of the bedroom helps limit allergen exposure. Bathing the pet with a special shampoo that removes dander also helps. Many individuals limit the amount of time they pet their animals, do not permit them to sit in their laps, and wash their hands frequently. Julia, who is allergic to cat dander but had a cat for many years, explains what she did: "I kept him out of my bedroom, keeping the door closed at all times. I tried not to hold him or touch him too much, which was very difficult. I always washed my hands after handling him, his belongings, and in litter clean up. I mentally made myself aware not to touch hands to eyes, and I took an antihistamine when I needed one."[54]

Coping with Outdoor Allergens

Individuals with pollen allergies face other challenges. Reducing exposure to these allergens is difficult but not impossible. One step many individuals take is to keep their windows and doors closed when pollen counts are high. This is especially helpful at night, since pollen counts peak in the early morning. According to Dr. Georgeson, "The highest pollen counts are from 4 am to 10 am. You'll wake up feeling symptoms after having a window open all night. You'll wake up with runny nose and tearing, which is no way to start a day."[55] Using an air conditioner also helps. Window fans, on the other hand, suck in outside air. Consequently, many people with pollen allergies avoid them.

And although it is hard to avoid going outdoors, on days when pollen counts are high, many individuals stay inside. When they do go outdoors, they often wear a protective mask while gardening or exercising and sunglasses, which help keep pollen out of the eyes. Once they return home, they can elimi-

A clerk displays items designed to protect the wearer from pollen, at a Tokyo department store in 2005.

nate exposure to pollen that clings to them by changing their clothes, showering, and washing their hair.

Another measure these individuals may take is planning vacation trips to places where pollen counts are typically low. This includes high elevations, the seashore, and urban areas. John explains: "My favorite vacation spot is Cannon Beach, Oregon. I love to walk on the beach, look at the ocean, and smell the salt air. The fact that I can breath better there is also great."[56]

Personal Care Challenges

People who are allergic to chemicals face other challenges. They often react to substances used in personal care products such as soap, cosmetics, deodorant, hair products, and body lotion by developing an itchy rash. Scratching the rash only causes it to become more inflamed and can break open the skin and lead to an infection. So, one important step these individuals can take is to avoid scratching. Instead, they can gently massage the area with their hands. They may also apply a topical antihistamine to ease the itching. Wearing loose fitting clothes that do not rub against the rash also helps keep itchiness down.

Of course, these individuals should also try to avoid exposure to allergy triggers. One way they can do this is by using hypoallergenic products. Such items, which include detergents, cleaning products, cosmetics, and personal care items, are free of perfumes and other chemicals that can trigger an allergic reaction in sensitive individuals. A physician who works for Almay, a manufacturer of hypoallergenic cosmetics, explains:

> Hypoallergenic means less likely to cause an allergic reaction.... [Hypoallergenic] products have been formulated and tested to minimize the possibility of an allergic reaction or irritation, making them safe for even the most sensitive skin. Fragrance-free refers to a product that has no added fragrance-masking agents added to alter the product odor....

Allergies and Kissing

In 2006 scientists investigated how long peanuts stay in a person's saliva after a person eats. To find out, the scientists had ten subjects eat a peanut butter sandwich. The scientists then collected samples of the subject's saliva at different intervals, including after the subjects had brushed their teeth and used mouthwash. Even after brushing their teeth and using mouthwash, all of the subjects had large amounts of peanut residue in their saliva immediately after eating the sandwich. After one hour, six out of seven had almost undetectable traces of the peanuts in their saliva. After four hours, none of the subjects had any detectable trace of the peanuts. As a result of the study, scientists say that people with peanut allergies should wait several hours before kissing someone who has eaten peanuts. Otherwise, they may unwittingly ingest peanut residue, causing an allergic reaction.

> Fragrance is the leading cause of allergic reactions in cosmetics. Products claiming to be hypoallergenic should be free of fragrance.[57]

Coping with Food Allergies

People with food allergies may do whatever it takes to avoid foods they react to. This can be challenging. It involves not only steering clear of the food itself but also other food items that use the offending food as an ingredient. For example, an individual who is allergic to eggs not only must avoid omelets and boiled eggs, but also cakes, breads, sauces, and noodles, to name just a few of the foods that contain eggs. Common food allergens can also be used in artificial food coloring, preservatives, oils, thickeners, edible starches, and protein powders, among other things.

Diligently reading food labels can help individuals with food allergies to avoid triggering allergens, but this is not easy. Allegra Cullen, who is allergic to peanuts, explains:

> By the time I was 3, I learned to read my first words. They were nut and peanut. My mom use to write the word 'peanut' on an index card and show it to me over and over again. Then when we were in the kitchen or grocery store, she would hand me food packages like cakes or gravy or potato chips and have me look for the word peanut. But at age 3, I certainly couldn't read words like lecithin, madelonas, food additive 322, hydrolyzed vegetable protein, marzipan, and emulsified ingredients, which all contain peanuts or nuts.[58]

The Food Allergen Labeling Consumer Protection Act (FALCPA), which was enacted in 2006, is helping to make label reading easier for people with food allergies. It requires that manufacturers list any of the eight most popular food allergens (peanuts, tree nuts, milk, eggs, wheat, soy, shellfish, and fish) found in a particular product in simple terms on the food label.

A list of common allergens is labeled on a box of Cheez-It crackers. Food manufacturers are required to label their products with these lists.

So, if a food contains the milk protein casein, for instance, the label indicates that the food contains casein, a milk product. Many manufacturers are also adding a warning if the food item is manufactured in a plant where any of the eight popular allergens are processed. This is to protect individuals from cross-contamination. Even if a food does not contain a particular allergen, if that allergen is present where the food is prepared, it is possible that cross-contamination can occur via cooking utensils or machinery. Or, dust containing traces of the allergen can settle on the food. For highly sensitive people, even minute traces of an allergen can be dangerous. For this reason, an individual who is highly allergic to peanuts, for example, will avoid eating a candy bar that is manufactured in a plant that also manufactures peanut-covered candies.

For the same reason, highly sensitive individuals may avoid being seated near people eating something that they are allergic to, since protein from the offending food can become airborne. Moreover, if someone eating the offending allergen gets the protein on their hands and then touches something, such as a cafeteria table, and then a sensitive individual comes in contact with the protein, this can cause a reaction. This is why some school children with food allergies eat at a separate cafeteria table or even in a different room from their peers. And classmates are often instructed not to bring snacks or party treats that contain the allergen into the classroom. Allegra explains that on the first day of school each year,

> I have to hand in this dreadful note. … The teacher stands in front of the whole class and reads this note out loud: "To whom it may concern: Please be advised that Allegra Cullen has a severe peanut and nut allergy. She cannot be exposed to any type of nut or nut ingredient. Please make sure you check all the labels for peanut/nut products or oils. Thank you." I feel so guilty because some kids sigh and say, "Awwwww."… From previous years, they know that they can no longer bring anything into the classroom if it has nuts. Then the nurse sends home a note telling the parents, too.[59]

A baker prepares flour made from rice at a special gluten-free bake house operated by Whole Foods Market. Rice flour is an alternative to wheat flour that can be used to make products safe for those with wheat allergies or gluten intolerance.

Getting Support

Enlisting the support of others is another way people with allergies cope. Friends, family members, coworkers, teachers, and school personnel all can help allergy sufferers reduce their chances of an allergic reaction. If a severe reaction does occur, their help can save lives. Many teachers, for example, are instructed in how to administer an EpiPen. Teachers and school nurses keep emergency plans on file for highly allergic students. These plans contain contact numbers and emergency care directions.

Even the government is lending a hand. A bill introduced in Congress in May 2007 provides grants to help schools implement plans to lower the risk of anaphylaxis in schools.

Family members help by not serving foods that a loved one is allergic to. Sometimes, this means keeping certain foods out of the house even if they are family favorites.

Airlines, also, are lending support. Some have stopped serving peanuts on all flights in order to protect passengers with peanut allergies. Others keep nuts off flights if they have been warned that a passenger has a nut allergy.

Eating in restaurants or at dinner parties presents more challenges. Unlike food labels, restaurant menus do not list all suspicious ingredients. So, individuals with food allergies must question the server about specific ingredients. Many even talk to the chef. Some make up cards listing all their food allergies, which they give to restaurant staff. They also warn their hosts about their allergies before attending dinner parties. Says Julia, who is allergic to nuts, "In restaurants, I always ask to have nuts omitted from foods and have the wait-person check if there are any nuts in the ingredients or cooking oils. Most of my close friends are very aware of my allergy and often prepare a nut-less portion. My friend Diane bakes special nut-less cookies just for me at Christmas."[60]

A medical alert necklace used for someone with a penicillin allergy. Necklaces and bracelets like these can warn a doctor of a patient's allergies even when they are unable to speak.

Being Prepared

Even when people with severe food allergies are diligent about avoiding allergens, emergencies can still arise. For them and other highly sensitive individuals, being prepared for an emergency can be the difference between life and death. It also reduces the emotional stress that living with the threat of anaphylaxis causes. These individuals, therefore, carry an EpiPen with them at all times. Many also instruct loved ones on how to use the device, in case they become too ill to inject themselves. Laura, a young woman with food allergies explains: "One of the most important things you can do when you go out is always carry your medicine, just in case. I forgot mine once, and I was very uncomfortable every time I thought about it not being with me. I was aware of its absence the entire night. It bothered me because I knew if I needed it, I wouldn't have it."[61]

Some individuals also wear a Medic Alert bracelet or necklace. It is engraved with a medical insignia on the front and a brief description of the person's diagnosis on the back, along with a telephone number. Upon calling the telephone number, which is answered twenty-four hours a day, first responders are given access to the individual's medical information. This ensures that even if individuals are unable to explain what their problem is, medical professionals will administer the proper treatment as soon as possible.

It is clear that when individuals act defensively to reduce both the chance of an allergic reaction occurring and to protect themselves if one does occur, they gain control over their lives. As a result, allergy sufferers can live happy, active lives just like people without allergies. Brooke, a teen with food allergies puts it this way: "My food allergies are only one part of me; they have never, and will never, control my life."[62]

CHAPTER FIVE

The Future of Allergies

Scientists are working on new ways to control allergies. These include developing new treatments, as well as investigating the sequence of events that causes an allergic reaction.

Desensitization for Food Allergies

Food allergies are one of the most dangerous types of allergies. Many scientists are investigating ways to lessen the threat food allergies pose to susceptible individuals. Since there is no treatment for food allergies, much of this effort centers on developing possible treatments.

Scientists at Duke University in Durham, North Carolina, are at the forefront of this research. They developed and are testing a promising form of immunotherapy for food allergies. The goal of the treatment is to desensitize individuals with peanut or egg allergies. But since injecting even a diluted food allergen directly into a sensitive person's bloodstream could be disastrous, the scientists developed an oral form of treatment in which patients are fed tiny, but increasing, amounts of the very food they are allergic to. Researchers theorize that, as with allergy shots, the subjects' immune systems will eventually build up a tolerance to the food allergen. Says researcher Wesley Burks, MD, "Our goals in treatment are the desensitization, to make them less sensitive and also to make the … allergy go away."[63]

To prove their theory, from 2004 to 2007, the scientists administered oral immunotherapy to seven children with an egg allergy and twenty-five children with a peanut allergy in

Elizabeth White mixes her daily dose of peanut powder with a fruit roll-up. She is part of a Duke University study that exposes her and other children with peanut allergies to gradually increasing amounts of peanuts, in an attempt to build up a tolerance for them.

two separate studies. Because the therapy is risky, the tests were conducted under tight medical supervision, and the subjects were monitored for hours after each treatment.

Depending on their particular allergy, the subjects were fed minute amounts of egg powder or peanut flour. The starting dose equaled one three-hundredth of a peanut or one one-thousandth of an egg. The amount was gradually increased until the subjects had some type of reaction. The subjects were then fed a dose just under the reactive dose every day for two weeks. Then the dosage was increased and so on. This procedure continued over a two-year period.

The egg study ended in 2006. At the conclusion of the study, four of the seven children in the egg group were able to eat two eggs without a reaction. The others were able to tolerate less than that amount, but more than before they started the therapy.

As of November 2007, the peanut study is still going on. After eighteen months, six of the twenty-five children were able to eat fifteen peanuts without a reaction. The researchers do not know if the desensitization will prove to be long lasting. To find out whether it is, subjects who have reached their maximum dosage are given a daily maintenance dose and monitored. Eventually, the daily maintenance dose will be stopped, and the subjects' reaction to the allergens will be tracked. At the same time, more trials are being conducted to test the therapy on a larger number of subjects. For now, the scientists are very hopeful. "What we're seeing is that they really are less sensitive to peanuts," says Burks. "If they accidentally have a bite of something with a peanut in it, they are not reacting…, What we have seen in almost all of them—they have had mild symptoms the first day or second time and then as you get a higher dose, you get less and less symptoms. That is why we are very encouraged by the results so far, because it really does appear that they are becoming desensitized."[64] Indeed, Burks predicts that desensitization will be a treatment for peanut allergies within a few years and that the same treatment should prove successful for other types of food allergies.

The researchers are not the only ones who are encouraged. Jennifer Parks, the mother of one of the test subjects, could not be happier with the results thus far. "It may not make him be able to eat a peanut butter sandwich some day," she explains, "but if it could keep him from dying from being in the same room with a peanut butter and jelly sandwich, just keep him from a life threatening situation, I feel like we won."[65]

Chinese Herbs to Treat Food Allergies

Scientists at Mount Sinai Hospital in New York City are investigating another way to help people with food allergies. By utilizing a mixture of eleven herbs traditionally used in China to fight inflammation, they hope to develop an herbal formula that blocks an anaphylactic reaction. In 2006, the scientists tested the herbal formula, known as food allergy herbal formula (FAHF-2), on mice, with promising results.

In this study, a group of ten mice whose immune system had been altered so that they were allergic to peanuts were administered a daily dose of FAHF-2 for seven weeks. Another group of ten peanut-allergic mice acted as a control. Both groups of mice were then fed peanut powder one, three, and five weeks after therapy ceased. All the mice in the control group developed severe anaphylaxis. The mice treated with FAHF-2 had no reaction even after five weeks. In addition, the mice's blood levels of IgE antibodies and histamine were measured before and after treatment. While the control group's levels remained constant, the treated group's levels declined gradually with treatment and stayed low five weeks after treatment.

The study established that FAHF-2 protected the mice against an allergic reaction for five weeks after treatment, but the scientists wondered if the effect would wear off. So, they

Traditional Chinese medicines—like the ones for sale at this apothecary in Macau, China—are being studied as possible allergy treatments.

reexposed the treated mice to peanuts forty and fifty weeks after treatment. The results were quite promising. After forty weeks, only one out of the ten mice reacted. After fifty weeks that number rose to three. At week sixty-six, the mice were once again treated with FAHF-2 and the experiment repeated itself. The retreatment provided protection for all the mice. Says researcher Dr. Kamal D. Srivastava, "This is a significant finding in terms of the duration of protection with a single course of treatment that can be taken orally, making it an effective and convenient treatment that can be administered at home."[66]

Despite these results, using FAHF-2 to treat food allergies in people will not occur anytime soon. Many experimental treatments prove effective on mice but do not work as well on humans. Moreover, because the herbal formula tastes bitter, it must be diluted with water. As a result, in order for humans to receive a sufficient dose of FAHF-2, they would have to take as many as twenty-four tablets per day, which may not be manageable. Scientists are working to solve this problem. When they do, human tests should begin.

Anti-IgE Therapy

Other scientists are taking a different approach. They are trying to develop a substance that can disrupt the chain reaction that triggers an allergic response. In 2003, researchers at the pharmaceutical company Tanox Inc. in Houston, Texas, developed a bio-engineered antibody known as TNX-901. It is composed of chemically altered IgG, the antibody the body produces to combat almost all foreign invaders. As a result of the alteration, TNX-901 identifies the IgE antibody produced by people allergic to peanuts as a foreign invader and blocks it from doing its job. It works by binding to the IgE antibodies, which keeps them from activating mast cells. As a result, the mast cells do not release histamine, and an allergic reaction is averted.

To test TNX-901, eighty-two people with peanut allergies were divided into four groups. Each group was given an injection of either a placebo, or 150mg, 300mg, or 450mg of TNX-901 once a month for four months. Before the treatment began,

Research is taking place around the world to develop new and better treatments for allergies. These test subjects at a Toyko, Japan, facility are reporting on their allergic reactions as they are exposed to cedar pollen.

the subjects underwent a food-challenge test to establish the level of their sensitivity to peanuts. The subjects' blood levels of IgE were measured before and after each injection, as well as periodically during the treatment period. Two to four weeks after the treatment ended, the subjects were once again given a food-challenge test. The baseline sensitivity level for all the subjects was between 176mg, or about half a peanut, to 436mg, a little more than one peanut. Sensitivity levels increased in all the groups, although not every subject showed improvement. It rose to an average of 710mg in the placebo group, 913mg in the group that received 150mg of TNX-901, 1650mg in the group that was given 300mg of TNX-901, and 2627mg in the group that was given 450mg of the medication. The latter is the equivalent of approximately nine peanuts. According to the researchers, "A 450 mg dose of TNX-901 significantly and substantially increased the threshold of sensitivity to peanut on oral food challenge from a level equal to approximately half a peanut to one equal to almost nine peanuts, an effect that should translate into protection against most unintended ingestions of peanuts."[67]

At the time of all the food-challenge tests, the subjects' blood levels of IgE were also checked. IgE levels decreased by between 72 and 89 percent in the subjects taking TNX-901. There was no change in placebo group.

Although these results are very encouraging, researchers make it clear that TNX-901 is not a cure for peanut allergies, nor is it a substitute for avoiding peanuts. But, since it decreases a person's sensitivity to peanuts, it does lessen the risk of anaphylaxis.

In an article on the National Jewish Medical and Research Center's Web site, researchers Hugh Sampson, MD, and Donald Leung, MD, discuss the study. "Anti-IgE therapy is not a cure for peanut allergy," Sampson explains. "We believe that patients would have to continue the injections for the benefits to persist and they still would need to be careful about what they eat. But, because the amount they could consume without serious reaction would be greatly increased, the fear of accidental ingestion that detracts from quality of life for many patients would be eliminated. These are very promising results."

Leung agrees: "Our results indicate that the anti-IgE antibody could become the first preventative medicine for peanut allergies. If future studies bear out this initial promise, anti-IgE could not only save lives, but help lift a cloud of fear that people with peanut allergies live under every time they eat."[68]

A number of other studies are under way to further test the effectiveness of TNX-901. And other scientists are working on developing a similar anti-IgE antibody targeting other allergens. In fact, one targeting cat dander is currently being tested on mice by researchers at the University of California–Los Angeles. It combines IgG with a protein taken from cat saliva. If all goes well, it is likely that anti-IgE therapy will be used to treat some allergies in the near future.

Allergy and Light

According to researchers at the Asthma Foundation of Western Australia, exposure to ultraviolet light may inhibit an allergic reaction. In 2007, the researchers altered the immune systems of laboratory mice in order to give them an allergy. Then they divided the mice into two groups. One group was exposed to ultraviolet light, then to a triggering allergen. The second group, which acted as the control, was exposed to the allergen but not the light. Then the researchers measured and compared the allergic response in the two groups. The mice that were exposed to ultraviolet light had fewer symptoms than the mice not exposed to the light.

Based on the study, the researchers think that ultraviolet light may inhibit the production of IgE, thereby suppressing an allergic reaction. Other studies are being conducted, including ones investigating ways to use ultraviolet light to treat allergies without causing other health issues linked to exposure to ultraviolet light, such as skin cancer.

An Allergy Vaccine

Scientists at Johns Hopkins University School of Medicine in Baltimore are also working on disrupting the sequence of events that leads to an allergic reaction. They are developing a vaccine that blocks the activation of T-helper cells (TH2).

TH2 cells are involved in ragweed allergies. When people who are allergic to ragweed encounter ragweed pollen, TH2 cells signal the body to produce IgE, which causes inflammation and an allergic response. The vaccine stops TH2 from responding to the allergen. According to head researcher Dr. Peter Socrates Creticos, "It's kind of like 'Let's Make a Deal'. You know the car is behind one door, but depending on which door you choose, you might not get the car. Well, now we know which door the car is behind. We know the cell [TH2] that can shut off the inflammation. Normally, the allergen wins the day, but now we redirect and shut it off."[69]

A researcher points to a bundle of pollen on a ragweed plant. Ragweed pollen is a common cause of allergies.

To create the vaccine, the scientists used DNA taken from harmless bacteria. Based on other studies, the scientists knew that the bacteria carry a DNA segment that the immune system recognizes as harmless. They theorized that if they created a vaccine that linked ragweed pollen and the DNA, they could trick the immune system into reacting to the bacteria rather than to the pollen. As a result, TH2 cells would not signal the release of IgE, and an allergic reaction would be deterred. University of California–San Diego researcher Dr. David Brode explains:

> The … vaccine links a ragweed particle to this bacterial DNA sequence. It's supposed to make the immune system of the person with ragweed allergy act just like the immune system of a person without ragweed allergy.… When this vaccine is injected into a patient, the immune

> system sees the ragweed component not as ragweed allergen but as [harmless] bacteria.... So the immune system is being fooled into making the correct response.[70]

Researchers tested the vaccine in 2006 on twenty-five adults with ragweed allergies. The subjects were divided into two groups. One group was administered one weekly injection of the vaccine every week for six weeks before the ragweed season began. The other group was given a placebo. Once the treatment ended, the subjects kept a detailed log of their allergy symptoms, recording each time they sneezed, their noses ran, or their eyes watered. Compared to the placebo group, the vaccine group experienced 60 percent fewer symptoms. Moreover, although no additional vaccine was administered, in the two years following the study, subjects in the vaccine group were still protected. Says Creticos, "We can provide relief, very effective relief that lasts for at least a couple of years with a very short-term regime. You won't have to take several medicines every day of ragweed season. You won't need shots every week for years. We can turn this disease off for years with a concise six-injection regime."[71]

In addition, unlike many allergy medications that affect multiple parts of the immune system, the vaccine is specific. It therefore is less likely to cause side effects. According to Rick Vinuya, an allergist at Providence Hospital in Southfield, Michigan, "The new vaccine is a smart bomb. It hones in on a specific target. The end effect is that the agent allows the treatment to be effective with less side effects."[72]

On the other hand, since the vaccine is specific to ragweed allergy, it does not protect individuals with multiple allergies. Scientists say, however, that changing the vaccine formula should make it effective against other allergens. With this in mind, researchers are currently working on developing similar vaccines against grass pollen, dust mites, and cat dander. And, tests of the ragweed vaccine on larger groups are on-going. If the results are equally impressive, the vaccine should become a treatment option in the future.

Hypnosis and Hay Fever

In 2005, a group of scientists at University Hospital in Basel, Switzerland, investigated whether self-hypnosis can decrease allergy symptoms. The study involved two groups of people with hay fever. During hay fever season, both groups were given antihistamine medication. In addition, one group was taught how to hypnotize themselves. While under hypnosis the subjects imagined themselves in a place free of allergens.

The scientists compared both groups' allergy symptoms over the course of two years. The comparison was based on measuring nasal congestion and the subjects' own analysis of their symptoms. The researchers found that the self-hypnosis group had up to one-third fewer allergy symptoms than the other group. In addition, the hypnosis group needed less medication than the control group.

The researchers are not sure whether the results were actually due to self-hypnotism or because the subjects believed that hypnotism would relieve their symptoms. In any case, the researchers say that since hypnotherapy does not cause side effects, it cannot hurt people with allergies to try it. In fact, there are tapes available that guide people with allergies in self-hypnotism.

Sublingual Immunotherapy

Although the allergy vaccine may someday help allergy sufferers to avoid the inconvenience of long-term allergy shots, it still entails multiple doctor visits and the administering of six injections. A new type of treatment known as sublingual immunotherapy (SLIT) eliminates injections and frequent doctor's visits. Like traditional immunotherapy, SLIT involves the administration of ever-increasing doses of triggering allergen extracts specially formulated for each patient, followed by treatment with a maintenance dose. Instead of the extract being administered via injection, a few drops are placed under the patient's tongue. The extract is retained under the tongue for a few minutes where it is absorbed into the bloodstream much like chewing tobacco. Whatever is left is swallowed.

Patients take the drops once or twice a day in their own homes. After about a month, when a maintenance dose is reached, the frequency of treatment decreases. The drops are tasteless and cause only one side effect, itching under the tongue. But because there is limited room under the tongue, the amount of each dose is significantly smaller than in immunotherapy. That means it takes longer to build up immunity with SLIT than with standard immunotherapy. With injections, patients usually experience allergy relief after one year of treatment. With SLIT it takes about two years to get the equivalent level of relief. But for people who fear injections, or those who do not have the time for traditional immunotherapy, SLIT offers another treatment option. Dr. Suzette Mikula of Georgetown University Hospital in Washington, D.C., explains:

> With SLIT, instead of weekly shots we have the patient administer their own drops from a dropper bottle under the tongue, everyday. It takes 2–3 years until they completely build their immune system and tolerance to things they're allergic to, which is slower than allergy injections. But using the drops has many benefits: they're easier for the patient who can administer their own drops at home instead of making a weekly doctor's appointment for a shot. It's a great alternative for adults and children who are afraid of needles, and for those who are highly reactive to shots. To date there have been no reports of any anaphylaxis or mortality due to the drops. Allergy shots carry a rare risk of death due to anaphylactic shock.[73]

Although SLIT is a new form of allergy treatment in the United States, it has been used to treat allergies in Europe for forty years. The therapy is gradually gaining support in the United States. Because it is not as effective as traditional immunotherapy, however, the treatment has not yet been approved

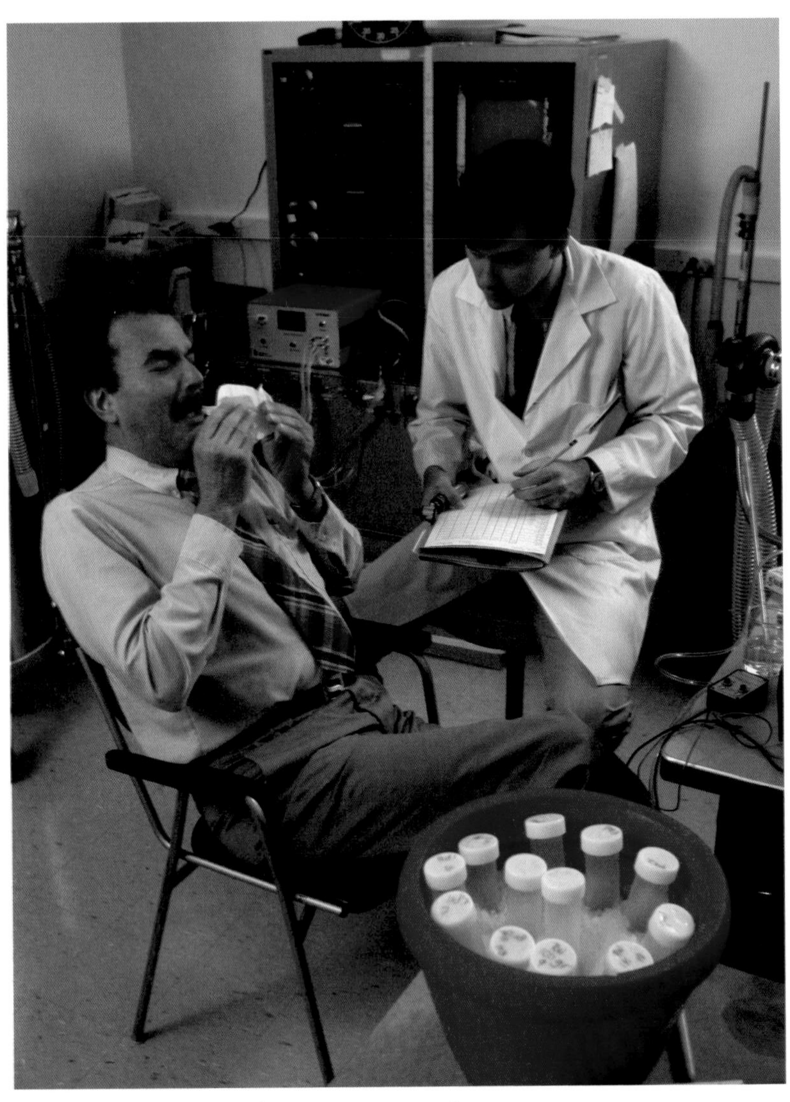

A doctor at Johns Hopkins University takes notes as a man sneezes.

by the FDA. The allergen extracts that are used in SLIT do have FDA approval, however. This allows physicians to prescribe the medication for sublingual use without breaking the law. Moreover, since a lot of research to verify the safety and effectiveness of the treatment has already been done, if the drops continue to gain popularity, it is likely that SLIT will be recognized by the

FDA and become a standard form of treatment. In the meantime, the therapy is offering relief for many individuals. Says Michael Gibson, who experienced debilitating headaches due to clogged sinuses caused by allergies, "I started the drops for dust and food allergies back in the fall of 2006. I know that six months after starting the drops I have had NO headaches.... I am doing great."[74]

Gibson is not the only allergy sufferer who has benefited from new allergy treatments. Treatments for food allergies, anti-IgE therapies, an allergy vaccine, and allergy drops are just a few of the many new developments in allergy research. Indeed, according to Dr. Peter Vadas, the director of allergy and immunology at St Michael's Hospital in Toronto, Canada, when it comes to controlling allergies, "the future looks bright."[75]

Notes

Introduction: A Widespread Problem

1. Quoted in The Food Allergy & Anaphylaxis Network, "A Reaction to College." www.faanteen.org/school/reaction_at_college.php.
2. Earl Mindell, *Earl Mindell's Allergy Bible*. New York: Warner Books, 2003, p. 7.
3. Quoted in Sean Flynn, "What You Can Do About Food Allergies," *Parade Magazine*, April 29, 2007, p. 29.
4. Family Allergy Clinic, "Frequently Asked Questions and Their Answers," www.allergiesrus.com/faq.html.
5. Quoted in Shelley Reese, "The Hidden Costs of Allergies," Business and Health. www.businessandhealth.com/'hostedfiles/features/allergiesatwork/physician /article03.
6. Quoted in The Food Allergy & Anaphylaxis Network, "Meet Alyssa," http://www.faanteen.org/about/alyssa.php

Chapter 1: What Are Allergies?

7. Frank K. Kwong and Bruce W. Cook, *The Complete Allergy Book*. Naperville, IL: SourceBooks, 2002, p. 102.
8. John, personal interview with author, Las Cruces, NM, July 25, 2007.
9. Melissa, e-mail interview with author, Hoboken, NJ, October 10, 2007.
10. John, personal interview.
11. Quoted in Healthology.com, "The Basics of Allergies," Webcast transcripts. www.healthology.com/hybrid/hybrid-autodetect.aspx?focus_handle=allergy-information&content_id=1719&brand_name=healthology.
12. Drgreene.org, Personal Stories, "Sam, 29 (dust, cats, bee stings)." www.drgreene.org/blank.cfm?print=yes&id=21&action=detail&ref=1314.
13. Quoted in Linda Gamlin, *The Allergy Bible*. Pleasantville,

NY: Reader's Digest, 2001, p. 54.
14. Quoted in Gamlin, *The Allergy Bible*, p. 60.
15. Quoted in Gamlin, *The Allergy Bible*, p. 8.
16. Quoted in Healthology.com, "The Basics of Allergies."
17. John, personal interview.
18. Quoted in Margaret Veach, "Latex Gloves Hand Health Workers a Growing Worry," *American Medical News*, October 13, 1997. www.latexallergylinks.org/AMNews.html.
19. Betty B. Wray, *Taking Charge of Asthma*. New York: Wiley, 1998, p. 2.

Chapter 2: Diagnosis and Conventional Treatment

20. Mindell, *Earl Mindell's Allergy Bible*, p. 14.
21. Katy Weaver, "Allergy Testing: Why It's Important and What You Can Learn," National Allergy, July 2007. www.natlallergy.com/article.asp?ai=295&bhcd2=1190767023#st1.
22. John, personal interview.
23. Weaver, "Allergy Testing."
24. Charles Atkins, "Food Challenges: Why Bother?" National Jewish Medical and Research Center, December 2006. www.njc.org/disease-info/diseases/ allergy/ about/diagnosed/food-challenge-why.aspx.
25. Mindell, *Earl Mindell's Allergy Bible*, p. 243.
26. Kwong and Cook, *The Complete Allergy Book*, p.127.
27. Kwong and Cook, *The Complete Allergy Book*, p.149.
28. American Association of Allergy, Asthma and Immunotherapy, "What Are 'Allergy Shots'?" www.aaaai.org/patients/publicedmat/tips/whatareallergyshots.stm.
29. Sarah, telephone interview with author, Dallas, Texas, September 26, 2007.
30. Quoted in CBS News, "Dustin Hoffman to the Rescue," July 27, 2004. www.cbsnews.com/stories/2004/07/27/earlyshow/health/main632072.shtml.
31. LaDonna Antoine-Watkins, "Unsung Heroes," Anaphylaxis Canada, www.anaphylaxis.ca/content/livingwith/heroes_ladonna.asp.
32. Healthology.com, "The Basics of Allergies."

Chapter 3: Alternative and Complementary Treatments

33. Drgreene.org., Personal Stories, "Penny, Age 35 (allergy shots)," www.drgreene.org/body.cfm?xyzpdqabc=0&id=21&action=detail&ref=1316.
34. Quoted in Gamlin, *The Allergy Bible*, p. 208.
35. Andreas Schapowal, "Butterbur Ze339 for Treatment of Intermittent Allergic Rhinitis." http://archotol.ama-assn.org/cgi/reprint/130/12/1381.pdf .
36. Quoted in Rick Ansorge, Eric Metcalf, and the editors of Prevention Health Books, "Ease Symptoms with Supplements," Prevention.com. www.prevention.com/cda/article/ease-symptoms-with-supplements/21ce50d1fa803110VgnVCM10000013281eac____/health/conditions.treatments/allergies.
37. Eucalyptus Nurseries, "Medicinal Uses," http://eucalyptus.co.uk/indepthguide/medicinaluses.asp.
38. Mindell, *Earl Mindell's Allergy Bible*, pp. 60–61.
39. Quoted in BBC News, "Vitamins Link to Asthma," December 7, 2001. http://news.bbc.co.uk/1/hi/scotland/1696485.stm.
40. Mindell, *Earl Mindell's Allergy Bible*, p. 66.
41. Quoted in Penn State University College of Medicine Web site, "An Apple a Day May Keep the Pulmonologist Away." www.hmc.psu.edu/agromedicine/toolbox/pulmonologist.htm.
42. Daniel K. Ng et al., A Double-Blind, Randomized, Placebo-Controlled Trial of Acupuncture for the Treatment of Childhood Persistent Allergic Rhinitis, *Pediatrics*, November 2004, p. 1242–7. http://pediatrics.aappublications.org/cgi/content/full/114/5/1242.
43. Gamlin, *The Allergy Bible*, p. 219.
44. Mindell, *Earl Mindell's Allergy Bible*, p. 26.

Chapter 4: Living with Allergies

45. Drgreene.org, Personal Stories, "Sam, 29 (dust, cats, bee stings)."
46. Quoted in Doug Donaldson, "Allergy-Proof Your Home," *Better Homes and Gardens*, March 2007, pp. 240–2.

47. Quoted in Healthology.com, "Living with Indoor Allergies," Webcast Transcript, March 3, 2000. www.healthology.com/hybrid/hybrid-autodetect.aspx?focus_handle=allergies&content_id=1723&brand_name=healthology.
48. Quoted in Healthology.com, "Living with Indoor Allergies."
49. Mindell, *Earl Mindell's Allergy Bible*, p. 140.
50. Sarah, telephone interview.
51. Quoted in Find Articles, "Evergreen Spores can Aggravate Allergies," http://findarticles.com/p/articles/mi_m1272/is_2703_132/ai_111403463.
52. Alan, telephone interview with author, Hewlett, NY, September 27, 2007.
53. Kwong and Cook, *The Complete Allergy Book*, p. 191.
54. Julia, e-mail interview with author, New York, NY, September 27, 2007.
55. Quoted in Donaldson, "Allergy-Proof Your Home."
56. John, personal interview.
57. Almay, "Dermatologist Advice," www.almay.com/pg/advice/dermatologistadvice.aspx?catid=100006&catnm=ExpertAdvice&subid=7&subnm=Dermatologist.
58. Allegra Cullen, "Guest Columnist Allegra Cullen, Age 12, on Peanut Allergy," Achoo Allergy and Air Products Web site. www.achooallergy.com/allegra-peanut-allergy.asp. Originally published in *Albany (NY) Times Union*, March 13, 2007.
59. Cullen, "Guest Columnist Allegra Cullen, Age 12, on Peanut Allergy."
60. Julia, e-mail interview.
61. FAAN Teen, "Going Out on the Town," www.faanteen.org/personalstories/going_out_on_the_town.php.
62. Food Allergy Initiative, "Essay from a Food Allergic Teenager." http://www.foodallergyinitiative.org/section_home.cfm?section_id=4&sub_section_id=5&article_id=64.

Chapter 5: The Future of Allergies

63. Quoted in ABC News, "Can Deadly Peanut Allergies Be Cured?" June 23, 2006, http://abcnews.go.com/print?id=2107158.

64. Quoted in ABC News, “Can Deadly Peanut Allergies Be Cured?”
65. Quoted in ABC News, “Can Deadly Peanut Allergies Be Cured?”
66. Quoted in Child Food Allergy, “Potential Herbal Formula Solution for Peanut Allergy,” March 15, 2006. www.childfoodallergy.com/archives/2006/03/potential_herba.html.
67. Donald Y. M. Leung et al., “Effect of Anti-IgE Therapy in Patients with Peanut Allergies, *New England Journal of Medicine*, March 13, 2003. http://content.nejm.org/cgi/content/short/348/11/986.
68. Quoted in National Jewish Medical and Research Center, “Medication Protects Patients with Peanut Allergies,” www.nationaljewish.org/news/y2003/peanut-allergies.aspx.
69. Quoted in Serena Gordon, “Vaccine May Ease Ragweed Allergies,” MedicineNet.com. www.medicinenet.com/script/main/art.asp?articlekey=76674.
70. Quoted in Daniel J. DeNoon, “Allergy Vaccine: 6 Shot Cure?” WebMD, October 4, 2006. www.webmd.com/allergies/news/20061004/allergy-vaccine-6-shot-cure?print=true.
71. Quoted in Gordon, “Vaccine May Ease Ragweed Allergies.”
72 Quoted in DeNoon, “Allergy Vaccine: 6 Shot Cure?”
73. Quoted in Georgetown University Hospital, “Allergy Relief Right Under Your Tongue?” April 24, 2007. www.georgetownuniversityhospital.org/body.cfm?xyzpdqabc=0&id=15&UserAction=PressDetails&action=detail&ref=154.
74. Quoted in Georgetown University Hospital, “Allergy Relief Right Under Your Tongue?”
75. Quoted in John Weisnagel, “Peanut Allergy: Where Do We Stand? Association of Allergists and Immunologists of Quebec. www.allerg.qc.ca/peanutallergy.htm.

Glossary

allergen: A harmless substance such as pollen or dust, that the body reacts to inappropriately.

allergic dermatitis: Redness, rash, or hives caused by an allergy.

allergic rhinitis: Nasal inflammation caused by an allergy.

allergy: An overreaction by the immune system to allergens.

alternative treatments: Therapies that are not widely accepted by conventional health-care professionals.

anaphylaxis: A severe full-body allergic response that can cause shock and death.

antibody: A protein produced by the immune system to defend the body against foreign substances.

antigen: A substance that activates the production of an antibody.

antihistamines: Medications that block the effect of histamines.

antioxidants: Natural substances that help protect the body against damage caused by oxidation, a process in which cells are weakened when they come in contact with oxygen molecules.

aromatherapy: A therapy in which individuals inhale vapors from warmed essential oils derived from plants that are believed to have medicinal properties.

atopy: A genetic predisposition to allergies.

complementary treatment: The practice of supplementing conventional treatments with alternative treatments.

cross-reactivity: A circumstance in which allergens share a similar protein, which causes an allergic reaction to both substances.

dander: A mix of animal saliva, skin, and hair.

decongestants: Medications that relieve nasal congestion.

dust mite: A microscopic creature related to ticks and spiders that lives by the millions in dust and bedding and whose droppings are a common allergen.

epinephrine: A medication that relieves the symptoms of anaphylaxis.

EpiPen: A device used to self-inject epinephrine.

flavonoids: A group of healthful substances found in fruits and vegetables.

hay fever: A common name for seasonal pollen allergies.

herbal therapy: Treatment with plants believed to have medicinal properties.

histamine: A chemical produced by the immune system to fight allergens.

immune system: The body's natural defenses from invading harmful organisms.

Immunoglobulin E (IgE): An antibody involved in all allergic reactions.

immunotherapy: Allergy treatment in which very small amounts of allergens are injected under the individual's skin to help desensitize the person to the allergens.

inflammation: The body's defense against germs, characterized by swelling, redness, and pain.

lymphocyte: A type of white blood cell that is involved in identifying foreign invaders of the body.

mast cells: Cells that line an individual's nose, bronchial tubes, skin, and gastrointestinal tract.

nasal corticosteroids: Medications administered in a nasal spray that relieve inflammation.

occupational allergy: An allergy to a substance that an individual is exposed to in the workplace.

over-the-counter medications: Drugs that can be purchased without a prescription.

placebo: A harmless medication, usually a sugar pill, often used in medical research.

pollen: A powder produced by flowering plants that is a common allergen.

radioallergosorbent test (RAST): An allergy test in which allergens are applied to a blood sample, which is examined for IgE antibodies.

seasonal allergies: Allergies that only occur during certain times of the year when a particular allergen, such as pollen, is circulating.

shock: A medical emergency caused by the collapse of the circulatory system.

sublingual immunotherapy (SLIT): Allergy treatment in which small amounts of an allergen are placed under the tongue.

systemic response: Affecting the whole body.

wheal: An itchy red bump similar to a mosquito bite.

Organizations to Contact

American Academy of Allergy, Asthma and Immunology

611 Wells St.
Milwaukee, WI 53202-3889
(800) 822-2762
Web site: www.aaaai.org

This professional organization offers information about allergies and asthma, including lists of doctors, allergy news, and an information hotline.

American College of Allergies, Asthma, and Immunology (ACAAI)

85 W. Algonquin Rd., Suite 550
Arlington Heights, IL 60005
(847) 427-1200
Web site: www.acaai.org

The college provides A-to-Z allergy topic information, lists of allergists, and the latest allergy and asthma news.

Asthma and Allergy Foundation of America

1125 Fifteenth St. NW, Suite 502
Washington, DC 20005
(800) 7ASTHMA (727-8462)
Web site: www.aafa.org

The foundation offers lots of information on allergies, including a multimedia library, Web links, pollen scores for major cities, and an allergy glossary.

The Food Allergy & Anaphylaxis Network

11781 Lee Jackson Hwy., Suite 160
Fairfax, VA 22033-3309
(800) 929-4040
Web site: www.foodallergy.org; www.faanteen.org

This organization promotes education, advocacy, research, and awareness about food allergies. Its teen Web site offers tips, personal stories, information, coping skills, and an e-newsletter. It also sponsors an annual conference.

Food Allergy Initiative

1414 Avenue of the Americas, Suite 1804
New York, NY 10019
(212) 207-1974
Web site: www.foodallergyinitiative.com

The initiative provides a wealth of information about food allergies, including the latest research, public policy information, and a newsletter.

For Further Reading

Books

Sherry Mabry Gordon, *Peanut Butter, Milk, and Other Deadly Threats: What You Should Know About Food Allergies*. Berkeley Heights, NJ: Enslow, 2006. Looks at what food allergies are, diagnoses, and current research.

Terry Allan Hicks, *Allergies*. New York: Marshall Cavendish, 2006. General information about allergies, including the history of allergies; has lots of photographs.

Steve Parker, *Allergies*. Chicago: Heinemann, 2004. Discusses what allergies are and how they are diagnosed and treated.

Alvin Silverstein, Virginia Silverstein, and Laura Silverstein Nunn, *Allergies*. New York: Franklin Watts, 2000. A simple but highly informative book about allergies.

Periodicals

Madeline Drexler, "Allergy Alert!" *Good Housekeeping*, May 2007.

Sean Flynn, "What You Can Do About Food Allergies," *Parade Magazine*, April 29, 2007.

Sarah Reistat-Long, "The Sneezy Season," *Real Simple*, April 2007.

Kristin Weir, "Crunch Time: The Urgent Search for a Cure for Deadly Peanut Allergies," *Current Science*, October 5, 2007.

Internet Sources

ABC News, "Can Deadly Peanut Allergies Be Cured?" June 23, 2006, http://abcnews.go.com/print?id=2107158.

CNN.com, "Living with Allergies," www.cnn.com/SPECIALS/2007/allergies/.

Mayo Clinic.com, "Allergy Skin Tests: Identify the Source of Your Allergies," www.mayoclinic.com/health/allergy-tests/AA00023.

Web Sites

Allergic Living (www.allergicliving.com). An online magazine that provides tips and information about living with allergies.

Allergy Haven (www.allergyhaven.com). Founded by the mother of a child with food allergies, this Web site provides lots of information about coping with food allergies.

EpiPen (www.epipen.com). Information on anaphylaxis, living with severe allergies, and how to use an EpiPen.

National Jewish Medical Research Center (www.njc.org). This Denver hospital specializes in treating allergies. Its Web site provides a wealth of information on allergies.

Index

Absenteeism, 11–12
Acupuncture, 52–54, *53*, 56
Air purifiers, 61
Allergen tests, *9*, *10*, 30–32
Allergens
  triggers, 28–30
  types, 17–18
Allergic reaction, 16–17, *17*
Allergic rhinitis, 9–10, 19
Allergic sensitization, 14
Allergy shots, 38–40, *39*, *44*
  See also Sublingual immunotherapy
Allergy-proofing, 59–63, *60*
Alternative and complementary treatments
  acupuncture, 52–54, *53*
  aromatherapy, 48–49
  defined, 44–46
  herbal treatments, 46–48, 76–78, *77*
  motivation for using, 43–44
  nutritional supplements and diet, 49–52
  safety, 55–58
Anaphylaxis
  anti-IgE therapy, 80
  epinephrine, 41–42, 72
  herbal creams, 57
  herbal treatment, 77
  Menses, 45
  physiology, 26–27
  prevention, 71
  shock, 24
  skin tests, 32
  sublingual immunotherapy, 85
Ancient history, 45
Antibodies, 13–14
Antigens, 13–14
Antihistamines, 35–36, *36*, 37
Anti-IgE therapy, 78–80
Anti-inflammatory herbs, 47
Antioxidants, 49–50
Antoine-Watkins, LaDonna, 42
Arelsmooth (soft drink), *50*
Aromatherapy, 48–49, 56
Asthma, 26, 54
Asthma Foundation of Western Australia, 81
Atopic people, 23–25
Avoidance, 34–35, 42, 59–66

Butterbur, *46*, 47, 56

Cat dander, 20, *64*, 64–65
China, ancient, 45, 52
Chinese herbs, 76–78, *77*
Christmas trees, 62–63
Cockroaches, 63
Contact allergies, 20–21, *25*
Cross reactivity, 22–23
Cullen, Allegra, 68, 70

Decongestants, 37, *37*
Dehumidifiers, 62
Desensitization, 74–76, *75*
Diagnosis
  food challenge tests, 33–34

skin tests, 30–32
triggers, 28–30
Diet. *See* Nutritional supplements and diet
Drechlera, *63*
Duke University research, 74–76
Dust and dust mites, *19*, 19–20, 61–62

Economic costs, 11, 12
Education, public, 12
Egg allergies, 74–75
Egypt, ancient, 45
Environmental issues, 25–26
Ephedra, 45, *45*
Epinephrine, *41*, 41–42
EpiPens, *41*, 41–42, 71, 72
Eucalyptus oil, 48, *49*

FAHF-2 treatments, 76–78
FALCPA (Food Allergen Labeling Consumer Protection Act), 68
Family history, 23–25
FDA (Food and Drug Administration)
Flavonoids, *50*, 51–52
Food Allergen Labeling Consumer Protection Act (FALCPA), 68
Food allergies
avoidance, 68–71
common food allergens, *22*
cross reactivity, 22–23
desensitization, 74–76, *75*
food challenge tests, 33–34, 79–80
kissing, 67
seriousness, 8, 9
Food allergy herbal formula (FAHF-2), 76–78
Food and Drug Administration (FDA), 44
Food challenge tests, 33–34, 79–80
Future of allergies. *See* Research

Genetics, 23–25
Gibson, Michael, 87
Gluten-free products, *70*
Government regulation, 44, 56–57
Greece, ancient, 45

Hay fever, 18–19, 84
Health issues, other, 9–10, 26
HEPA filters, 61
Herbal treatments, 46–48, 55–57, 76–78, *77*
High efficiency particle air (HEPA) filters, 61
Hippocrates, 45
Histamine, 16
History, 45
Hypersensitivity, 13
Hypnosis, 84
Hypoallergenic products, 67–68

Immune system, 13–15
Immunotherapy, 38–40, *39*, 43, *44*, 84–87
Incidence statistics, 10, 40
Indoor allergens, 59–63
Ingested allergens. *See* Food allergies
Inhalant allergies, *18*, 18–20, 65–66, 81–83, 84
Insect venom, 20–21, *21*, 45
International incidence, 40

Johns Hopkins University

School of Medicine, 81, *86*

Kissing, 67
Knowledge, 12

Labeling, 68–69, *69*
Latex allergies, *25*, 26
Legislation, 68
Life threatening conditions, 8–9, 21, 26–27, 40, 41–42
Light therapy, 81
Lymphocytes, *14*, 15

Maternal diet, 50–51
Medical Alert jewelry, *72*, 73
Medical conditions influenced by allergies, 9–10, 26
Medications, 35–38, 43
Menses, 45
Mold, 62–63, *63*
Mount Sinai Hospital research, 76–78

Nasal corticosteroids, 38
National Jewish Medical and Research Center, 80
Nettles, 47–48, *55*, 56
Neutrophils, 15, *15*
Nutritional supplements and diet, 49–52, 56, 57–58

Occupational allergies, *25*, 26

Parks, Jennifer, 76
Peanut allergies. *See* Food allergies
Personal care products, 66–68
Pet dander, 20, 64–65
Physiology
  allergic reaction, 16–17
  anaphylaxis, 26–27
  antihistamines, *36*
  immune system, 13–15
Pollen, *17*, *18*, 18–19, *29*, 65–66, 81–83, *82*
Pollen counts, 33
Poplar wool, *18*
Productivity loss, 12
Protective wear, 65–66, *66*

Radioallergosorbent test (RAST), 32, 33
Ragweed, *29*, 81–83, *82*
RAST (radioallergosorbent test), 32, 33
Research, *79*, *86*
  anti-IgE therapy, 78–80
  Chinese herb treatments, 76–78
  desensitization, 74–76
  sublingual immunotherapy, 84–87
  ultraviolet light treatment, 81
  vaccines, 81–83
Restaurants, 71
Rhinitis, 9–10, 19

School absenteeism, 11
Scratch test, 31–32
Seasonal pollen allergies, 18–19, 65–66
Secondary conditions, 26
Shock, 24, 27, 41, 85
  See also Anaphylaxis
Side effects of medications, 36, 37, 43
Skin contact allergies, 20
Skin tests, *9*, *10*, 30–32
SLIT (sublingual immunotherapy), 84–87
Social costs, 11–12
Statistics, incidence, 10, 40
Sublingual immunotherapy,

84–87
Susceptibility, 11, 23–25
Symptoms, 8–9, 16–17

Tanox Inc., 78
Tests. *See* Diagnosis
TNX-901, 78–80
Traditional Chinese medicine, 76–78, *77*
Treatments
  anaphylaxis, 41–42
  antihistamines, 35–36
  anti-IgE therapy, 78–80
  avoidance, 34–35, 42, 59–66
  decongestants, 37, *37*
  desensitization, 74–76, *75*
  herbal, 46–48
  history, 45
  hypnosis, 84
  immunotherapy, 38–40, *39*, *44*
  nasal corticosteroids, 38
  sublingual immunotherapy, 84–87
  ultraviolet light, 81
  See also Alternative and complementary treatments
Triggers, 28–30

Ultraviolet light therapy, 81
University of California-Los Angeles, 80

Vaccines, 81–83
Vacuuming, *60*, 61
Vitamins, 49–51, 57–58

Weil, Andrew, 48
White blood cells, *14*, 15, *15*
Work issues, 11–12

Picture Credits

Cover: Image copyright Bronwyn Photo, 2007. Used under license of Shutterstock.com.
3D4Medical.com/Getty Images, 14
AP Images, 10, 25, 29, 30, 35, 41, 70, 75, 79, 82
Martha Cooper/National Geographic/Getty Images, 86
Macduff Everton/The Image Bank/Getty Images, 77
© Erik Freeland/Corbis, 22
Rich Frishman/Time Life Pictures/Getty Images, 9
Gale Cengage Learning, 21, 36, 56
Innerhofer/StockFood Creative/Getty Images, 55
© 2008 Jupiterimages, 37, 44, 60
© Mark Karrass/Corbis, 53
Toshifumi Kitamura/AFP/Getty Images, 50
Natalia Kolesnikova/AFP/Getty Images, 18
Koichi Kumagaya/Sebun Photo/Getty Images, 46
Dr. Dennis Kunkel/Visuals Unlimited/Getty Images, 17
Spike Mafford/Stockbyte/Getty Images, 72
Dr. Darlyne A. Murawski/National Geographic/Getty Images, 19
Scott Olson/Getty Images, 69
© Bob Sacha/Corbis, 39, 64
David Scharf/Science Faction/Getty Images, 63
© Scott T. Smith/Corbis, 45
Yoshikazu Tsuno/AFP/Getty Images, 66
© Visuals Unlimited/Corbis, 15
Matthew Wakem/Aurora/Getty Images, 49

About the Author

Barbara Sheen is the author of more than forty nonfiction books for young people. She lives in New Mexico with her family. In her spare time, she likes to swim, walk, cook, read, and garden. Like so many other people, she has seasonal allergies.